Stitch by Stitch

Volume 20

TORSTAR BOOKS

NEW YORK · TORONTO

Stitch by Stitch

TORSTAR BOOKS INC.
41 MADISON AVENUE
SUITE 2900
NEW YORK, NY 10010

Knitting and crochet abbreviations

approx = approximately
beg = begin(ning)
ch = chain(s)
cm = centimeter(s)
cont = continue(ing)
dc = double crochet
dec = decreas(e)(ing)
dtr = double triple
foll = follow(ing)
g = gram(s)
grp = group(s)
hdc = half double
    crochet

in = inch(es)
inc = increas(e)(ing)
K = knit
oz = ounce(s)
P = purl
patt = pattern
psso = pass slipped
    stitch over
rem = remain(ing)
rep = repeat
RS = right side
sc = single crochet
sl = slip

sl st = slip stitch
sp = space(s)
st(s) = stitch(es)
tbl = through back of
    loop(s)
tog = together
tr = triple crochet
WS = wrong side
wyib = with yarn in
    back
wyif = with yarn in front
yd = yard(s)
yo = yarn over

A guide to the pattern sizes

		10	12	14	16	18	20
Bust	in	32½	34	36	38	40	42
	cm	83	87	92	97	102	107
Waist	in	25	26½	28	30	32	34
	cm	64	67	71	76	81	87
Hips	in	34½	36	38	40	42	44
	cm	88	92	97	102	107	112

Torstar Books also offers a range of acrylic book stands, designed to keep instructional books such as *Stitch by Stitch* open, flat and upright while leaving the hands free for practical work.

For information write to Torstar Books Inc., 41 Madison Avenue, Suite 2900, New York, NY 10010.

Library of Congress Cataloging in Publication Data
Main entry under title:

Stitch by stitch.

Includes index.
1. Needlework. I. Torstar Books (Firm)
TT705.S74 1984   746.4   84-111
ISBN 0-920269-00-1 (set)

9876543

© Marshall Cavendish Limited 1985

Printed in Belgium

Contents

Crochet / COURSE 89

More about broomstick crochet

In the last course we showed you how to work the basic broomstick crochet stitches and some of the variations which can be worked on these stitches. In this course we show you how to vary the patterns with the use of different crochet stitches or yarns and how to introduce new yarns and colors into the patterns.

There is no reason why you should confine yourself to making only blankets, stoles or scarves, which need no shaping, since very attractive tops, jackets, ponchos and capes can be made from strips, rectangles or squares, which can be sewn or crocheted together in the same way as for a patchwork fabric (see Volume 16, page 24). Our pictures use the 5-loop broomstick

pattern, which can be twisted from left to right, or vice versa (see Volume 19, 27), but you can, of course, use any of loop variations shown in Volume 19, 29, working the correct number of stit into the loops.

Introducing new yarn or changing colors

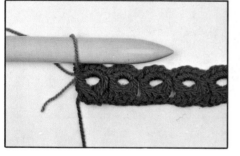

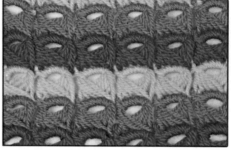

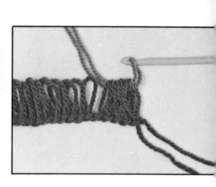

1 To change color or yarn on a loop row, draw the new yarn through the last stitch worked in the single crochet row by drawing the yarn through the last two loops of the last stitch in the usual way. Tighten the yarn at the edge of the work by pulling the two loose ends together once the loop has been placed on the pin.

2 The next loop row can then be worked with the new color. Here a loop row and a single crochet row have been worked in a sequence of three colors for a simple striped pattern.

3 To change the color or introduce a new ball of yarn on a single crochet row, drop the old yarn and draw throug a loop of the new yarn, taking it throug the center of the looped group, which been twisted in the correct direction.

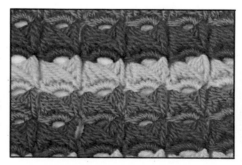

4 Make one chain with both the working end and the loose end of yarn before working the single crochet into the loops in the usual way.

5 In this sample the colors have been changed on every single crochet row, using three colors in rotation, together with a medium hook and ¾in (20mm) pin.

6 In this sample colors have been chan on every row so that the loops and the single crochet rows are worked in different colors. Break off the yarn at th end of every row and introduce it agair when needed.

ern variations

appearance of broomstick crochet
rns can be changed considerably by
ng the stitches worked between the
. Be careful to work only small
bers of rows between the loops to
nt the fabric from becoming dis-
d at the edges, and remember that
e loops are worked on the wrong
of the fabric, so that you should work
even number of rows between each
row. Try the samples in a knitting
ted or Aran-style yarn, so that you
see the structure of the patterns
e progressing to more textured or
yarns.

1 In this sample doubles instead of single crochets have been worked between the loops. Work the first row of loops in the normal way, then turn and insert the hook through the first group, drawing through a loop and making three chains instead of one, to count as the first double.

2 Now work 5 doubles into the first group before continuing to work in doubles across the row, making sure that the doubles are worked firmly to prevent this row from spreading outward.

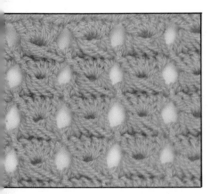

e completed doubles and loop pattern
es an open fabric which would be
for a lacy shawl if worked in
e yarn.

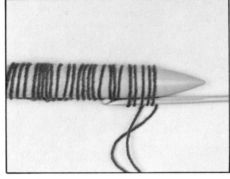

4 When working with a fine yarn or crochet cotton, you may find it more satisfactory to insert the hook through the loops while they are still on the pin. Insert the hook from right to left through the loops in the normal way, leaving the remaining loops on the pin.

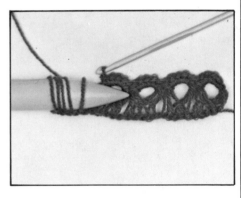

5 Remove the working loops from the pin and complete the group in the normal way. Continue to take each group off the pin separately so that unworked loops are held on the pin until needed.

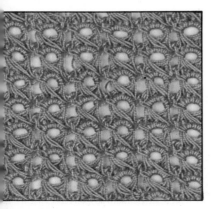

edium-weight crochet cotton and a
hook make a beautiful, lacy fabric as
wn here. Use single crochets or half
les between the loops to hold the
s together firmly.

7 Be careful when working larger strips between the loops to ensure that you maintain a straight edge. Here three doubles rows have been worked between the loops so that the resulting crochet piece bulges at the edges.

8 To avoid making a misshapen fabric, as shown in step 7, work either single crochets or half doubles between the loops, depending on the yarn used. Experiment before making a complete fabric to ensure that your pattern works satisfactorily with the yarn to be used.
continued

Mike Berend

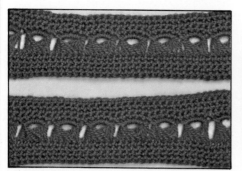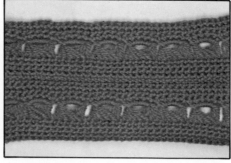

9 To make wide strips between the loops with either double stitches or other crochet patterns, you can make the broomstick crochet in separate strips and sew or crochet them together. Make strips with plain crochet worked on each side of the loops as shown above.

10 Overcast the pieces together on the wrong side of the fabric to make a seam that is invisible on the right side of the work.

11 Alternatively the pieces can be crocheted together on the right side of the work to make a feature of the seam. Use the strips either horizontally, as shown in step 10, or vertically as show here.

Three sample patterns

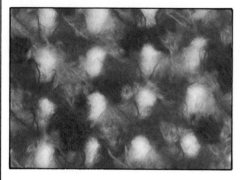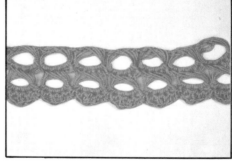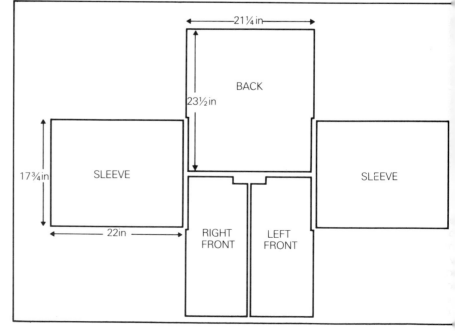

1 Variegated mohair yarn worked on a large pin and hook with doubles worked between the loop rows makes a loose, open fabric.

2 A fine crochet cotton edging made by working two loop rows followed by a simple shell worked onto the last single crochet row.

3 A small pattern worked on a small hook and ⅝in (15mm) pin in a sport y to make a light, warm fabric which co be used for a baby's blanket.

Chinese-style jacket

Broomstick crochet makes a pretty textured jacket.

Sizes
To fit 34-36in (87-92cm) bust.
Length, 23½in (59.5cm).
Sleeve seam, 22in (56cm).

Materials
36oz (1000g) of a bulky yarn
Size J (6.00mm) crochet hook
1in (25mm) pin
6 toggles

Gauge
2 groups measure approx 2¾in (7cm) across. One patt repeat—6 rows— measures 4in (10cm) in depth.

draw through a loop, place this loop on pin, *insert hook into next dc, yo and draw through a loop, place this loop on pin, rep from * to end. 85 loops. Remove loops from pin.

5th row Insert hook from right to left through first 5 loops, 1ch, 5sc into loops, *insert hook from right to left through next 5 loops, 5sc into loops, rep from * to end.

Turn. 85sc and 17 groups.

6th row as 3rd.

7th row as 4th.

The 2nd to 7th rows form the patt. Rep them 3 times more, then work 2nd–5th rows again.

Shape for armholes

Next row Patt over first 11 groups. Fasten off. Rejoin yarn to base row and work crossed dc over 11 groups to match first side. Fasten off.

Right front

Work as given for back until 12 rows have been worked, so ending with a 5th row.

Shape neck

Next row Patt to within last group, turn. Patt 3 rows. Fasten off.

Shape for armhole

Rejoin yarn to base row at lower edge and work crossed dc over 11 groups. Fasten off.

Left front

Work as right front, reversing shaping.

Sleeves

Base row Using size J (6.00mm) hook make 80ch. Work first row as given for back, then cont in patt until the 2nd row of the 5th patt has been worked. Fasten off. Rejoin yarn to base row and work a row of crossed dc. Fasten off.

Collar

With RS facing join yarn to right front neck and using size J (6.00mm) hook work 1sc into each st along front neck to within last st, 2sc, 1ch and 2sc into corner, (2sc into side of dc, 1sc into next st, 3sc into loop sp, 1sc into next st) around neck to beg of left front neck, 2sc, 1ch and 2sc into corner, 1sc into each st to front edge. Turn. Work 9 rows in sc, working 2sc into 1ch at each corner. Fasten off.

Frog fastenings

Using size J (6.00mm) hook and yarn double make 3 × 4¾in (12cm) lengths of ch.

To finish

Join shoulder seams. Set in sleeves, then join side and sleeve seams, reversing seam for 5½in (14cm) for cuff. Turn cuff back. Twist and sew lengths of chain to form fastenings, then sew to right front of jacket. Sew on toggles.

row Using size J (6.00mm) hook e 85ch loosely for side edge.

w Transfer loop on hook to 1in m) pin. Insert hook into 2nd ch from o and draw through a loop, place op on pin, *insert hook into next o and draw through a loop, place on pin, rep from * to end. ps. Remove loops from pin.

2nd row (RS) Insert hook from left to right through first 5 loops, 1ch, 5sc into loops, *insert hook from left to right through next 5 loops, 5sc into loops, rep from * to end. Turn. 85sc and 17 groups.

3rd row 3ch, *skip next sc, 1dc into next sc, 1dc into sc that was skipped – 2dc crossed –, rep from * to end. Turn.

4th row Transfer loop on hook to pin. Insert hook into 2nd dc from pin, yo and

*Crochet toys
*Stuffing
*Simple shapes
*Stitch Wise: raised flower pattern
*Patterns for a snail and an alligator

Crochet toys

Crochet toys can be fun to make, and they make attractive, inexpensive gifts.

The cost of the materials can be kept to a minimum by using left-over lengths of yarn and making features from pieces of fabric or felt that you may have in your scrap bag.

Traditional toys, such as teddy bears, rabbits, pandas, etc., can all be made in crochet, as can more unusual examples of bird, animal and insect life. Embroidery can be used instead of—or in addition to—felt to make features. Embroidery stitches are also useful for marking hooves, feet, hands or claws on an unshaped piece where additional shaping would be too complicated.

You should always use single crochet for the main fabric to ensure a smooth, fabric which will cover the stu completely, although more tex stitches can be used to highlig particular section or create a tex effect. For example, crochet loops Volume 13, page 10) could be used polar bear or sheep or to imitate the s on the back of a porcupine.

Stuffing

Stuffing the different shapes correctly is a very important part of making a toy successfully and should not be hurried, since it is the only way to ensure that you end up with a perfect shape.

Synthetic stuffing, soft flock, which is an ideal stuffing for babies' toys, batting, small pieces of plastic foam and even woolen garments or old, clean stockings or pantyhose cut into small pieces can all be used to stuff toys.

Choose a washable stuffing and yarn for a baby's or toddler's toy which will need frequent washing; this will prevent disappointment later. A baby's toy should be stuffed with something quite soft and pliable, while larger, firmer toys can be stuffed with fiberfill or plastic foam pieces.

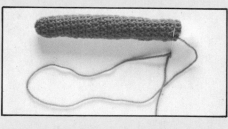

1 The simple tubular shapes described in this issue are stuffed by inserting small pieces of stuffing into the lower end and working upward until the shape has has been completely filled. Mold the shape while stuffing so that the stuffing is evenly distributed throughout.

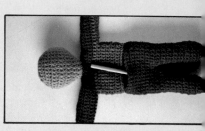

2 If the toy is made from several differe pieces or parts, for example, legs and a head in addition to a body, start by stuffing the outer points. Using small pieces of stuffing, start with the feet ar push the stuffing firmly into the lowes point with a small piece of doweling. Do not stuff a small child's toy too firm or it will become stiff and inflexible.

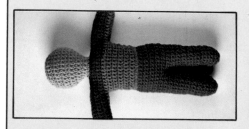

3 Continue to stuff the outer sections first, progressing to the arms, nose, head and so on, before finally stuffing the body. Always mold the shape as you work and use small pieces of stuffing each time so that it is evenly distributed throughout and a good shape is achieved.

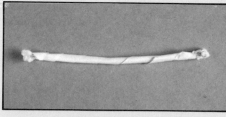

4 If you wish to strengthen a narrow piece such as an arm or a leg, use a pipe cleaner inserted into the crochet. Twist the pipe cleaner so that it forms a loop at each end and bind it with tape.

5 Wrap batting/fiberfill around the wire and bind once more, catching the tape with a few stitches to hold it in pla Insert the strengthener into the limb, pushing extra stuffing down each side necessary to complete the limb. The strengthener can be bent double to for two legs. The same method can be use to strengthen a long neck on an animal such as a horse or giraffe.

...ple shapes

...e of the most appealing toys are made
...g simple shapes like the ones shown
...lume 19, page 16. With the addition
...rs, legs and different faces, a number
...ifferent creatures can be made from
...basic shape. The "sausage" shape
...d to make the snail and the alligator
...wn on page 10 is extremely versatile.

1 When making the basic shape, make
sure that the center seam is sewn firmly
and neatly together on the underside of
the creature so that it will not be seen
once the toy has been completed.

2 Use a similar tube for the snail's
shell, rolling it up from one end and
making sure that there are no creases
in the crochet.

...old the spiral in position by catching
...two sections at intervals with small,
...t stitches. Always sew seams as
...ly and strongly as possible when
...ing toys so that they do not
...ntegrate as soon as the are used.
...ecessary, use a stronger thread than
...one used to make the main fabric,
...g a matching or harmonizing color.

4 Use a ladder stitch to hold the shell in
position on the main body. This stitch—
in which one small stitch is worked into
the lower, then the upper, section each
time—is a useful stitch for sewing on
heads, ears, arms, etc., since each
stitch can be pulled tight once it has
been worked, so making the joining
invisible.

5 Here the coil or spiral has been used
horizontally instead of vertically and
combined with a tube and embroidery
to make a simple turtle.

Fred Mancini

Stitch Wise

Raised flower pattern

Make a number of chains divisible by 6 plus 1 and 1 extra
turning chain.
1st row (RS) 1hdc into 3rd ch from hook, 1hdc into each ch
to end. Turn.
2nd row 2ch to count as first hdc, 1hdc between each hdc to
end. Turn.
3rd and 4th rows Work 2nd row twice.
5th row 2ch, (1hdc between next 2hdc) 3 times, * work 6hdc
around stem of next hdc on 4th row, turn and work 6dc around
stem of preceding hdc on 4th row, join with a sl st to first dc,
turn again and cont along row, work (1hdc between next
2 hdc) 6 times, rep from * to end, finishing (1hdc between next
2hdc) 3 times. Turn.
6th-10th rows Work 2nd row 5 times.
11th row 2ch, (1hdc between next 2 hdc) 6 times, *work 6dc
around stem of next hdc on 10th row, turn and work 6dc
around stem of preceding hdc on 10th row, join with a sl st to
first dc, turn again and cont along row, work (1hdc between
next 2hdc) 6 times, rep from * to end. Turn.
12th and 13th rows Work 2nd row.
The 2nd to 13th rows form the patt and are rep throughout.

Snail and alligator

They are not always popular creatures, but we're sure you will warm to our charming snail and alligator.

Snail

Size
18 × 11¾in (46 × 30cm).

Materials
3oz (75g) of a knitting worsted in first color (A) for body
2oz (50g) in 2nd color (B) for shell
Size F (4.00mm) crochet hook
Stuffing
2 long beads and 2 small round beads

Gauge
19sc and 24 rows to 4in (10cm) worked on size F (4.00mm) hook.
19hdc and 16 rows to 4in (10cm) worked on size F (4.00mm) hook.

Body
Using size F (4.00mm) hook and A, make 41 ch.
Base row 1sc into 3rd ch from hook, 1sc into each ch to end. Turn. 40sc.
Patt row 1sc into each sc to end. Turn.
Rep the patt row until work measures 18in (46cm). Fasten off.

Shell
Using size F (4.00mm) hook and B, make 44ch.
Base row 1hdc into 3rd ch from hook, 1hdc into each ch to end. Turn. 43 hdc.
Patt row 2ch to count as first hdc, 1hdc into each hdc to end. Turn.
Rep the patt row until work measures 29in (74cm) from beg. Fasten off.

To finish
Join long seam of body. Gather one end, stuff firmly, then gather other end.
Join long seam of shell. Gather one end, stuff firmly, then roll and sew shell and sew to body as shown in picture.
Make antennae from beads and sew to body.
If making snail for a very small child, leave off antennae.

Alligator

Size
Length, 18in (46cm).

Materials
2oz (50g) of a knitting worsted in first color (A) for body
4oz (100g) in 2nd color (B) for legs and eyes
Size F (4.00mm) crochet hook
Scraps of white felt for eyes
2 safety eyes for toys
12in (30cm) of rick-rack braid

Gauge
19 sc and 24 rows to 4in (10cm) worked on size F (4.00mm) hook.
19 hdc and 16 rows to 4in (10cm) worked on size F (4.00mm) hook.

Body
Using size F (4.00mm) hook and A, make 41ch.
Base row 1hdc into 3rd ch from hook, 1hdc into each ch to end. Turn.
Patt row 2ch to count as first hdc, 1hdc into each hdc to end. Turn.
Rep the patt row until work measures 14in (35cm) from beg.
Cut off A. Join on B.
Cont in sc for head, until work measures 18in (46cm). Fasten off.

Legs (Make 2)
Using size F (4.00mm) hook and B, make 41 ch.
Base row 1sc into 2nd ch from hook, 1sc into each ch to end. Turn.
Patt row 1sc into each sc to end. Turn.
Rep patt row for 6in (15cm). Fasten off.

Eyes (make 2)
Using size F (4.00mm) hook and B, make 27ch. Work base row as given for legs, then rep the patt row until work measures 2in (5cm). Fasten off.

To finish
Join long seam of body. Fold body in half, placing seam at center, and join one short end. Stuff firmly, then gather other end.
Join long seam of each leg. Gather one end, stuff firmly, then gather other end. Sew legs to body, sewing through center to form two legs on each side. Join short ends of eyes. Gather one open end.
Cut two circles of felt, each 1¼in (3cm) diameter. Sew felt to gathered ends of eyes, then position safety eyes on felt. Attach eyes, stuff firmly, then gather other end. Sew rick-rack braid around head section.

*Making a crochet glove puppet
*Making different features
*Patterns for four animal glove puppets

Making a crochet glove puppet

Instructions are given on page 14 for a basic glove puppet, along with ideas for making a cat, dog, rabbit and pig. Once you have made the basic shape, you can see how easy it is to use this shape to make a large number of different animals by changing the features and facial expressions.

The head can be stuffed with batting to achieve a firm, rounded shape, or left empty, depending on the effect you wish to achieve. The step-by-step pictures show how to make a stuffed and unstuffed head, using the same basic shape.

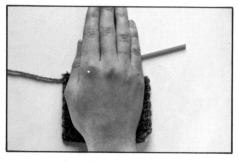

1 The basic glove is made in knitting worsted and worked in single crochet. (See page 14 for detailed instructions on how to work the glove.) Work the first part straight before shaping the arms. This section should be wide enough to take the hand comfortably.

2 To increase for the arms, producing smooth edge, you work the increases inside the edges at the beginning and of the row.

3 Each arm is made separately by working over six stitches at each side of the main section. By increasing at the outer edge and decreasing at the inner edge on every row, you make the arms slope outward as shown here.

4 Paws shaped at each end of each arm can be worked in the same color as the head, or one side can be worked in a mohair or angora yarn to indicate a soft pad as shown here.

5 With RS facing, rejoin the yarn to the next unworked stitch and complete the head on these center stitches between the two arms. Make sure that the top shaping is worked smoothly and even so that you obtain a good head shape.

6 You will find that you obtain the best results if you embroider the eyes, nose and any other parts of the face on the basic shape **before** the front and back are sewn together.

7 The puppet is made from two pieces of an identical shape. Place sections together and work around edges using single crochet in the same color.

8 The head can be stuffed for a rounde firmer shape. Turn the body wrong side out and stuff the head lightly with fiberfill, so that it is soft and pliable. Ma sure that there is a hole in the center of the stuffing for your fingers.

ake a strip of loose, half doubles fabric
sisting of 8 half doubles rows with 15
hes in each row to hold the stuffing
ace.

10 Sew the strip to the base of the head
on the inside. Slip stitch the strip to the
main section, catching the stitches
under one loop only so that they do not
show on the right side of the fabric. Work
all around in this way.

11 Push the crochet strip up into the
head so that the fingers can be inserted
into the head. Turn the glove right side
out and mold the head into shape.

king different features

can use felt or embroidery to suggest
s, noses and mouths, depending on
results you wish to achieve. For a
e three-dimensional effect on—for
mple—ears, make separate shapes
crochet and sew them to the head. In
eral, the head should be in single
het for a firm shape, but you could
small areas of loop stitch to represent
texture of fur.

expression of the puppet can be
ed by changing the position or size
e eyes, the direction of the mouth and
way the ears or hair are placed. Our
uctions on page 14 show you how
ake a dog, cat, pig and rabbit, but
ese little puppets can be made using
rent ears, hair and facial expressions.

1 Felt or embroidery can both be used for
the eyes. Felt eyes can be made with more
than one piece and color. Above, cat's
eyes have been made with a white
lozenge shape and a dark slit in the center.
Below, dog's eyes have been made with
a light outer circle and dark inner circle.

2 To embroider eyes on the puppet, use
satin stitch and one dark color. Eyelashes
can be worked effectively with
embroidery, graduating the lengths all
around the eye as shown here.

ore texture is achieved by making the
e with embroidery rather than felt,
ch could create only a flat shape. Work
r the position for the nose until you
e built up the correct shape for the
pet being made.

4 The direction in which an embroidered
mouth is made can alter the appearance
of the puppet considerably. Above, the
downward sloping mouth is suitable for a
dog, while the upward-sloping mouth
below is more suitable for a cat.

5 Whiskers are quite easy to make. Thread
a short piece of yarn onto a darning
needle and thread the yarn through both
sides of the face, leaving a loose end on
each side as shown here.

continued

Fred Mancini

6 Pointed ears can be made from a rectangle of crochet. Fold two corners to the center and sew them in place on the back of the ear. Open the ears at the center and insert a small piece of stuffing into the ear for a furry effect if desired.

7 Rounded ears can be made by working single crochet on both sides of a length of chains, working three single crochets into the top to create a rounded edge. For a furry lining, embroider chain stitches at center in angora or mohair.

8 There are several different ways of making fur. One of the easiest is to wc the appropriate section in loop stitch page 1506), leaving the loops uncut f curly look, or cutting the loops for a straight effect.

Four animal glove puppets

A menagerie of puppets to keep the children occupied on rainy—or sunny—days.

Sizes
To fit an average 6-10-year-old child's hand.
Length, 7½in (19cm).
Width from tip to tip, 7¾in (20cm).

Materials
Knitting worsted
Cat *1oz (25g) in each of blue, maroon, gray and white*
Left-over lengths of black yarn for embroidery
2 buttons
Dog *1oz (25g) in each of yellow, green, beige and medium brown*
Left-over lengths of black, pink and maroon yarn
2 buttons
Pig *1oz (25g) in each of yellow and pink*
Left-over lengths of white, black and maroon yarn
2 buttons
Rabbit *1oz (25g) in each of black, maroon and white*
Left-over lengths of blue yarn
4 buttons
Size F (4.00mm) crochet hook

Gauge
20sc and 22 rows to 4in (10cm) worked on size F (4.00mm) hook.

Basic glove puppet

Make 16ch.
Base row 1sc into 2nd ch from hook, 1sc into each ch to end. Turn. 15sc.
Next row 1ch to count as first sc, 1sc into each sc to end. Turn. Rep last row

13 times more.
Next row 1ch, 2sc into first sc, work to last sc, 2sc into last sc. Turn.
Next row 1ch, 1sc into each sc to end. Turn.
Rep last 2 rows until there are 27 sts, ending with an inc row.
First arm
Next row Work across first 6 sts, turn.
Next row 1ch, (insert hook into next st and pull yarn through) twice, yo and pull through all loops on hook—called dec 1 –, 1sc into each sc to last sc, 2sc into last sc. Turn. 6 sts.
Next row 1ch, 1sc into each sc to end. Turn. Rep last 2 rows twice more.
Next row 1ch, (dec 1) 3 times.
Next row Dec 2. Fasten off.
Second arm
Skip center 15 sts, rejoin yarn to next st, 1sc into same st, 1sc into each of last 5 sts. Turn.
Next row 1ch, 2sc into first sc, 1sc into each of next 3sc, dec 1 over last 2sc. Turn.
Next row 1ch, 1sc into each sc to end. Rep last 2 rows twice more. Complete as given for first arm.
Head
Rejoin yarn to first of 15sc at center. Work 9 rows in sc. Dec one st at each end of next 5 rows. 5 sts rem. Fasten off. Make another section in the same way. Place sections tog and work in sc around sides in appropriate color.

Cat

Using blue, work first 15 rows of lower body. Change to maroon and work 11 rows of increasing for arms.
Work first 5 rows of arms in maroon, then remainder in white. Rejoin maroon to upper body and work 2 rows, then change to gray to complete head.

Ears (make 2)
Using gray, make 10ch.
Base row 1sc into 2nd ch from hook, 1sc

into each sc to end. Turn. 9sc.
Work 5 more rows in sc. Fasten off.
Fold corners over to make a point and sew to top of head.

Features
Using black, embroider eyes, eyelash nose and mouth. Thread 5 short lengt white behind nose to form whiskers.

Collar
Using white, sew around neck in blan stitch. Return in opposite direction, working blanket stitch over top to forr a link patt.

Straps (make 2)
Using blue, make 30ch. Attach to top blue "skirt" at front and back. Sew buttons to end of front straps.

Dog

Using green, make 16ch.
Base row 1sc into 2nd ch from hook, into each ch to end. Turn.
1st row 1ch, 1sc into each of first 3sc, changing to yellow on last st, (3sc in yellow, 3sc in green) to end. Turn.
2nd row (3sc in green, 3sc in yellow) last 3 sts, 3sc in green.
3rd-4th rows (3sc in yellow, 3sc in green) to last 3 sts, 3sc in yellow.
5th-6th rows As 2nd.
7th-8th rows As 3rd and 4th.
Cut off green. Cont in yellow, working first 5 rows of arms in yellow, then remainder in beige.
7th-8th rows As 3rd and 4th.
Cut off green. Cont in yellow, working first 5 rows of arms in yellow, then remainder in beige.
Rejoin yellow to upper body and work rows, then change to beige to comple head.

Ears (make 2)
Using medium-brown, make 10ch.
1st row 1sc into 2nd ch from hook, 1s

into each of next 7ch, 3sc into last ch,
then working along other side of ch,
work 1sc into each of rem 8ch. Turn.
Next row 1ch, 1sc into each of first 8sc,
2sc into next sc, 1sc into next sc, 2sc
into next sc, 1sc into each sc to end.
Turn.
Rep last row twice more. Fasten off.
Gather flat end and attach ears to head.

Features
Using black, embroider eyes and nose.
Using pink, embroider mouth.

Suspenders (make 2)
Using maroon, make 30ch. Attach to top
of patterned "pants" at front and back.
Sew buttons to end of front suspenders.

Pig

Using yellow, work up to last 12 rows
except arms, which have first 5 rows in
yellow, then rest in pink. Work remainder
of head in pink.

Ears (make 2)
Using pink, make 3ch. Join with a sl st
into first ch to form a circle.
1st round Work 8sc into circle.
2nd round Work 2sc into each sc. 16sc.
3rd round (1sc into next sc, 2sc into
next sc) all around. 24sc.
4th round (2sc into next sc, 1sc into
each of next 2sc) all around. 32sc.
Fasten off.
Fold ears in half and attach to head.

Features
Using black, embroider eyes.
Snout Using needle and length of double
pink, place needle between and just
below eyes. Wind yarn several times
around needle, then secure at each end.
Using black, embroider nostrils.

Collar
Using white, make 31ch.
Next row 1sc into 2nd ch from hook, 1sc
into each of next 2sc, *3ch, sl st into last
sc worked, 1sc into each of next 3ch,
rep from * to end. Fasten off.
Attach collar around neck.
Using an extra piece of yarn make a bow
at neck.

Rabbit

Using black, make 16ch.
Base row 1sc into 2nd ch from hook, 1sc
into each ch to end. Turn.
1st row 1ch, 1sc into each of first 3sc,
changing to white on last st, (3sc in
white, 3sc in black) to end.
2nd row (3sc in black, 3sc in white) to
last sts, 3sc in black.
Rep last row 4 times more.
Change to maroon for rest of body.
Work first 5 rows of arms in maroon, then
complete arms in white.

Rejoin maroon to upper body and work 2
rows. Complete head in white.

Ears (make 2)
Using white, make 11ch.
1st row Work 1sc into 2nd ch from hook,
1sc into each of next 8ch, 3sc into last
ch, then working along other side of ch,
work 1sc into each of 9ch. Turn.
2nd row 1ch, 1sc into each of first 9sc,
3sc into top sc, 1sc into each of rem
9sc. Turn.
3rd row 1ch, 1sc into each of first 10sc,

3sc into top sc, 1sc into each of rem 1
Fasten off.
Fold base of each ear to center, sew
down, then attach to head.

Features
Using blue, embroider eyes. Using bl
embroider nose and mouth.
Work a row of blanket stitch in black
center front for "jacket" opening. Sew
buttons to "jacket."
Thread black yarn around neck for "ti
Make bow at center front.

Simon Butcher

*Embroidery on crochet
*Embroidery on a single
  crochet fabric
*Embroidery on a filet
  crochet background
ˣPattern for an embroidered
  filet curtain and tray cloth

broidery on crochet

 technique combines plain crochet
ics and embroidery stitches to create
oossed or decorated fabrics. It takes a
ain amount of practice to achieve
sfactory embroidery results.
his course we show you how to work
oroidery on a plain single crochet
kground, as well as the more difficult
nnique of working around a central

motif on a filet crochet background to
create a beautifully embossed filet lace
fabric.
Most of the simpler embroidery stitches
can be used on a dense background,
since the crochet fabric can be used in
the same way as the usual woven fabric
background, although you must be very
careful to work the stitches evenly and

neatly so that the crochet fabric does not
become pulled out of shape.
Embroidery on filet crochet is more
complex and uses only simple needlepoint
stitches worked into the blocks. This
technique can prove difficult to master,
but with practice you can produce
superb embroidered lace fabrics with a
wide variety of uses.

broidery on a single crochet fabric

 can use either knitting or tapestry
 for the embroidery, depending on
 heavy you want it to be. Knitting
 ns, especially the bulkier varieties, will
 a thickly-textured effect worked on
 of a single crochet background, so
 a flatter-looking design tapestry yarn
 referable.
ic designs can be worked "freehand,"
ctly onto the fabric, but for more
nplicated embroidery designs, it is
isable to plan the pattern on graph
er first, making each square on the
er represent one stitch in the back-
und fabric. Mark the embroidery
tern on the paper, using symbols to
resent the various stitches to be used.

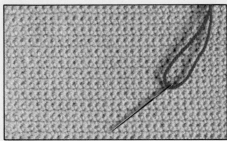

1 To try the various stitches, make a
piece of single crochet fabric with
knitting worsted and a size F (4.00mm)
hook, so that the resulting crochet is
dense and even. Begin by working a
simple freehand flower design on the
background fabric, using knitting worsted
for the embroidery.

2 Most embroidery stitches are best
worked through the upper surface of the
stitches (so that the yarn does not go
through to the back).
To work satin stitch begin by taking the
yarn through the center of two or three
stitches holding the end of yarn in place
with thumb and index finger of left hand.

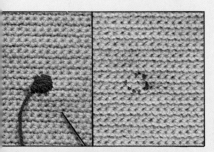

old the loose end at the front of the
rk so that you can work over it. Now
rk a petal in satin stitch, taking the
n from left to right and through the
face of the crochet stitches each
e (left), so that the embroidery is
ually invisible on the wrong side of
work (right).

4 Hold the yarn with the thumb and
index finger of the left hand while it is
being pulled through the crochet fabric,
to prevent it from being pulled too
tightly through the fabric, which would
cause the background to become
distorted. Try to avoid working between
rows of stitches, since this can create a
hole in the background fabric.

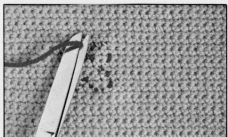

5 To fasten off the yarn, run it through
stitches at the back of the petal or flower
and cut it off close to the stitches.

continued

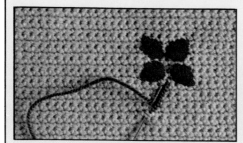

6 To work stem stitch take the yarn diagonally or vertically across the fabric through the surface of the stitches, in the same way as when working satin stitch, holding each previous stitch with the thumb and index finger of left hand so that the yarn is not pulled through too tightly , which would distort the fabric. Always make sure that the stitches are worked lightly and evenly, and **never** pull the yarn tightly through the fabric.

7 Use French knots to create flower centers in contrasting colors or small flower heads as shown here. As for the other stitches, take the needle only part-way into the fabric, and complete the knot as close as possible to the position where needle is first brought through.

8 Use chain stitch to create shapes or outline blocks worked into the croche' Here a simple crochet shamrock patter has been worked in chain stitch across background piece of single crochet an outlined with cross-stitch to make a simple border pattern.

Embroidery on a filet crochet background

This technique takes time and practice to perfect, since working the embroidery around a filet motif can prove tricky, but once mastered, it creates beautifully decorated lace fabrics. Use stranded embroidery floss for the embroidery, with a medium-weight crochet cotton for the filet background, thus creating a fabric which is strong enough to support the embroidery. Knitting yarn would be too heavy for the embroidery, and crochet cotton does not have the required stranded effect when worked onto the surface of the filet background. You can use contrasting colors, as shown in our steps, for the embroidery. Alternatively, interesting effects can be achieved by working both the embroidery and the background in the same color, so creating textural contrast without the distraction of different colors.

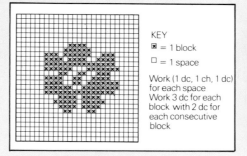

KEY

⊠ = 1 block
☐ = 1 space

Work (1 dc, 1 ch, 1 dc) for each space
Work 3 dc for each block with 2 dc for each consecutive block

1 This simple chart will help you to practice your embroidery before progressing to the more intricate patterns used for the curtain and tray cloth featured on page 20. Use a fine filet mesh for this pattern, in which 1 double, 1 chain and 1 double are worked for each space, with 3 doubles worked for each block and 2 doubles worked in each consecutive block. See Volume 7, page 22 for detailed instructions.

2 Make a sample piece of crochet from the chart using a size C (3.00mm) hoo and suitable crochet cotton. Work at le three rows of spaces all around the motif so that the embroidery can be worked satisfactorily onto the background.

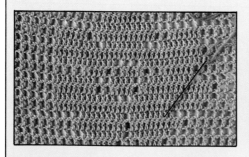

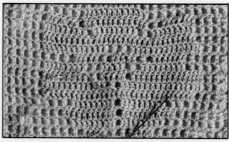

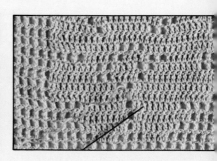

3 Choose a contrasting embroidery floss for this sample so that you can see how the stitches are worked. Thread the yarn on a fairly large tapestry needle.

4 To work around the motif, start at the inner corner of one petal, bringing the yarn through the middle of the fabric (see step 2 of "Embroidery on a single crochet fabric") and up to the right side, about ¼in (5mm) from edge of motif.

5 Take the yarn over the edge of the motif, into the space at the edge, and bring the needle up through the background fabric once more, next to the first stitch.

Fred Mancini

ntinue to work around the edge of
lower, keeping the stitches as close
ossible, and working over the same
e twice if necessary to make sure
the edge is completely covered.
the thumb and index finger of the
hand, lightly hold the previously-
ked stitches and the yarn being drawn
ugh, so that the tension remains
and the fabric smooth.

7 Here the flower has been outlined with
embroidery floss all around each petal.
The embroidery stitches need not be
exactly the same length all around, since
different length stitches can be used to
emphasize the shape of a petal or
indicate shading.

8 The center can also be outlined in this
way. Use either the same yarn or a
contrasting color to accentuate the
center of your flower as shown here.

nbroidered filet curtain and tray cloth

ng home a touch of gracious living with this delicate curtain
d matching tray cloth.

rtain

51 in (76×130cm).

erials
700yd (1600m) of a lightweight
 mercerized crochet cotton
 skeins each of stranded
 embroidery floss in shaded yellow
 and shaded orange
ize C (2.50mm) crochet hook
apestry needle

ge
ps in width and 16 rows to 4in (10cm)
ked on size C (3.00mm) hook.

nake
g size C (3.00mm) hook make
ch.
e row 1sc into 6th ch from hook,
, skip next ch, 1dc into next ch – 1
t formed –, (3ch, skip next 3ch,
into next ch – 1 lacet sp formed –,
, skip next ch, 1sc into next ch,
, skip next ch, 1dc into next ch – 1
t formed) 7 times, 3ch, skip next
, 1dc into next ch – 1 lacet sp formed –,
h, skip next sp, 1dc into next sp)
imes – 50 sps formed –, (3ch,
next 3ch, 1dc into next ch – 1 lacet
ormed –, 2ch, skip next ch, 1sc
next ch, skip next ch, 1dc into next
– 1 lacet formed) 8 times. Turn.
row 6ch, 1dc into next dc – 1lacet sp
ked over 1 lacet –, (2ch, 1sc into

next lacet sp, 2ch, 1dc into next dc – 1
lacet worked over 1 lacet sp –, work (1
lacet sp, 1 lacet) 7 times, 50 sps, (1
lacet, 1 lacet sp) 8 times, working last
dc into 3rd of the 5 ch. Turn.
Beg 2nd row of chart foll instructions at
side of chart, cont in patt as set, working
lacet patt at each end and flower patt
from chart over center 50 sps until the
162nd row has been worked. Now cont
in lacet patt, work 4 rows of sps over
center 50 sps, then work 3 rows of dc
across all sts. Fasten off.
Edging Rejoin yarn to lower edge at
corner, *2ch, 1dc into next sc, 1ch, 1dc
into next dc, 1ch, 1dc into center ch of
next 3ch, 2ch, 1sc into next dc, sl st into
next ch, sl st into next sc, 2ch, 1dc into
next dc, 1ch, 1dc into center of next
3ch, 1ch, 1dc into next dc, 2ch, 1sc into
next sc, sl st into next ch, sl st into next dc,
2ch, 1dc into center of 3ch, 1ch, 1dc into
next dc*, 1ch, 1dc into next sc, 2ch, 1sc
into next dc, sl st into next 2ch, 2ch, 1dc
into next dc, 1ch, 1dc into next sc, 1ch,
1dc into next dc, 2ch, 1sc into center of
3ch, sl st into next ch, sl st into next dc,
rep from * to *, (1ch, 1dc into next dc, 2ch,
1sc into next dc, sl st into next ch, sl st into
next dc, 2ch, 1dc into next dc, 1ch, 1dc
into next dc) 10 times working last dc
into center of 3ch, 1ch, 1dc into next dc,
2ch, 1sc into next sc, sl st into next ch,
sl st into next dc, 2ch, 1dc into center of
3ch, 1ch, 1dc into next dc, 1ch, 1sc into
next sc, 2ch, 1sc into next dc, sl st into
each of next 2ch, 2ch, 1dc into next dc,

1ch, 1dc into next sc, 1ch, 1dc into next
dc, 2ch, 1sc into center of 3ch, sl st into
next ch, sl st into next dc, rep from * to *,
1ch, 1dc into next sc, 2ch, 1sc into next
dc, sl st into each next 2ch, 2ch, 1dc into
next dc, 1dc into next sc, 1ch, 1dc into
corner. Fasten off.
Join yarn to top corner of curtain (with
right side facing) and working down side
work 2sc into each sp working a picot
into every 3rd sp as foll: 1sc, 3ch, sl st
into first 3ch, 1sc, rep this to bottom
edging, *2sc into 2ch sp, 2sc into next sp,
1 picot, 2sc into next sp, 2sc into 2ch,
1sc into center sl st. Rep from * along
lower edge, then work up 2nd side to
match first side. Fasten off. Use shaded
yellow for stem and center and shaded
orange for outer edge of 2 outer flowers,
reverse colors for center flower. Work
embroidery as shown working blanket
stitch to outline flower and stem, and
stem stitch and French knots at center.

Tray cloth

Size
11 × 15¾in (28×40cm).

Materials
350yd (320m) of a lightweight
 mercerized crochet cotton
1 skein each of stranded embroidery
 floss in shaded yellow and
 shaded orange
Size C (3.00mm) crochet hook
Tapestry needle

Gauge
17 sps in width and 16 rows to 4in
(10cm) worked on size C (3.00mm) hook.

To make
Using size C (3.00mm) hook make 94ch.
Base row 1sc into 6th ch from hook, 2ch,
skip 1ch, 1dc into next ch, – 1 lacet
formed – 3ch, skip next 3ch, 1dc into
next ch – 1 lacet sp formed –, (1ch,
skip next ch, 1dc into next ch) 20 times –
20 sps formed –, 1dc into each of next
6ch – 3 blks formed –, (1ch, skip next ch,
1dc into next ch) 14 times – 14 sps
formed –, 3ch, skip next 3ch, 1dc into
next ch – 1 lacet sp formed –, 2ch,

skip next ch, 1sc into next ch, 2ch,
1dc into last ch – 1 lacet formed. Turn.
1st row 6ch, 1dc into next dc – 1 lacet sp
formed –, 2ch, 1sc into next lacet sp,
2ch, 1dc into next dc – 1 lacet formed –,
work 14 sps, 1ch, skip next dc, 1dc into
next dc – 1sp worked over 1blk, 2blks,
1dc into next sp, 1dc into next dc – 1blk
worked over 1sp –, work 19 sps, 2ch,
1sc into next sp, 2ch, 1dc into next dc – 1
lacet formed –, 3ch, 1dc into 3rd of the
5ch – 1 lacet sp formed. Turn.
2nd row 1 lacet, 1 lacet sp, 19 sps,
3 blks, 15sps, 1 lacet sp, 1 lacet. Turn.
Beg with 3rd row, cont in patt as set,
working from chart, until the 62nd row

has been worked.
Next row 2sc into first sp, 3ch, sl st into
3rd ch from hook – picot formed –, *2sc
into each of next 2 sps, work a picot
rep from * to end, do not turn but
work along side edge working 4sc into
corner sp, (work a picot, 2sc into each
of next 2 row ends) to corner, complete
rem two edges in the same way, sl st
into first sc. Fasten off.
Using shaded yellow for stem and cent
of flower and shaded orange for outer
edge of flower, work embroidery (as
shown opposite), working blanket stitc
to outline flower and stem, and stem sti
and French knots at center of flower.

CURTAIN

74-137
Rep 10-73 once

50 sps

□ = 1 sp   ☒ = 1 blk

TRAY CLOTH

Base row

⊽ = 1 lacet   □□ = 1 lacet sp   □ = 1 sp   ☒ = 1 blk

Pompom pizzazz

Give an old sweater — or s[...]
or knitted gloves — a fun, r[...]
look with a scattering of p[...]
poms. They're easy to m[...]
and a good way to use up l[...]
over balls of yarn.

Materials

Sweater, scarf, or other garment
Assorted balls of sport or
worsted-weight yarn in various
colors
Small piece of cardboard
Drawing compass or small round
object the diameter of pompom
Large tapestry needle

1 Using the compass or small round object, draw a circle the desired diameter of the finished pompom on the cardboard. Draw another circle identical to the first. Cut out the circles.

2 Cut a hole about ¾in (2cm) in diameter in the exact center of each cardboard disk.

3 Place the two disks together and wind yarn up over the edges and down through the hole, covering the disks thickly and evenly. When the hole is nearly full, thread the yarn into a large tapestry needle to force it through.

4 Slip scissors through the yarn at th[...] edge, between the two disks, and carefully cut the yarn all around.

5 Pull the disks apart slightly and, us[...] a separate piece of matching yarn, tie[...] strands tightly around the middle. Pul[...] disks away.

6 Fluff the ends of the yarn and trim[...] them, if necessary, to get a smooth, round shape, leaving the ties untrimm[...]

7 Use the tying yarn to sew or tie ea[...] pompom to the garment.

* Circular designs in hairpin lace crochet
* Linking strips to form a circle
* Linking and crocheting strips to form a circle
* Stitch Wise: more methods for joining strips
* Pattern for a tablecloth

ular designs in hairpin lace crochet

you have learned how to make strips
airpin lace with different center
es and some methods of joining,
an go on to work circular designs.
n lace can be used for circular
ns by working and joining strips of
g lengths. The strips can either be
together, crocheted together or
d with a combination of linking and
et—as in the tablecloth on page 27.

Openwork crochet can be used to join
the strips; and by using a fine crochet
cotton, you can make pretty, delicate
mats and tablecloths.
When you are working a strip with a
large number of loops, you will find that
the hairpin fork or loom becomes very full.
When it is full, remove the loops from the
prongs and place the last three or four
loops back on the prongs and continue
working as before, as shown at right.

ing strips to form a circle

rst strip, to be placed at the center, is
d on one side with crochet. This
is joined along its short edges to
a circle, and each subsequent strip
ed to the preceding strip.

1 Using a 1½in (40mm) hairpin loom,
size E (3.50mm) crochet hook and sport
yarn, make a strip of hairpin lace, working
single crochet at center, with 48 loops on
each side.
Work crochet edging along one side of
strip by inserting crochet hook into first
8 loops, joining on yarn (here we have
used a contrasting color for clarity) and
working 1 single crochet. This single
crochet links the first 8 loops of the strip
together.

2 Now work *1 chain, insert hook into
next 8 loops and work 1 single crochet,
repeat from * to end of strip. Work
1 chain, then join chain to first single
crochet with a slip stitch to form a circle.
The crochet edge is at the center.

continued

Fred Mancini

23

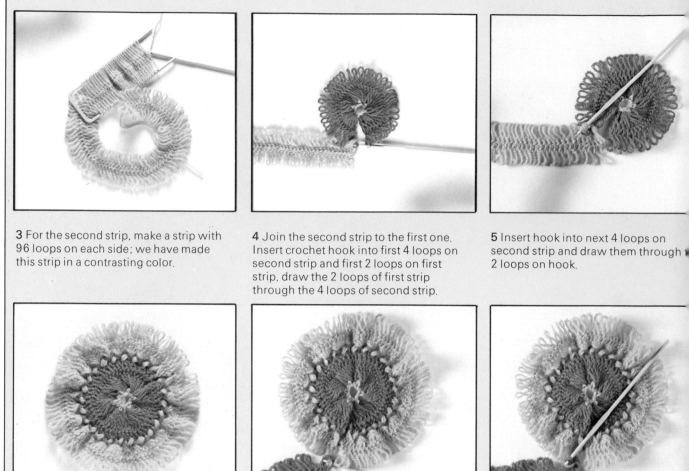

3 For the second strip, make a strip with 96 loops on each side; we have made this strip in a contrasting color.

4 Join the second strip to the first one. Insert crochet hook into first 4 loops on second strip and first 2 loops on first strip, draw the 2 loops of first strip through the 4 loops of second strip.

5 Insert hook into next 4 loops on second strip and draw them through ⬤ 2 loops on hook.

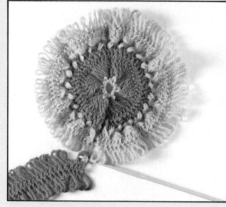

6 Repeat steps 4 and 5 to end of strip. Join strip into a circle by joining first and last loops and center stitches.

7 For the third strip, make a strip with 144 loops on each side. Join this strip to second strip by inserting hook into next 3 loops on third strip and next 2 loops on second strip and drawing the 2 loops of second strip through the 3 loops of third strip.

8 Insert hook into next 3 loops on thir strip and draw through the 2 loops on hook.

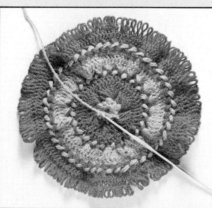

9 Repeat steps 7 and 8 to end of strip. Join strip into a circle as before.

10 To close the center, join yarn to one stitch on crocheted edge of first strip and work 3 chains to stand as the first double, then work 1 double into each stitch all around.

11 Draw yarn through the top of each double and gather tightly and secure. This completes the circle.

king and crocheting strips to form a circle

tablecloth on page 27 uses strips of
ng lengths which are joined together
the linking method and a decorative
het joining.
we show in detail how to join the
strips. The 10 chains between the
nd and third strips have been worked
contrasting yarn to emphasize the
l.

1 Make and join 2 strips as described in "Linking strips to form a circle."
The third strip is joined to the second strip by working crochet into the loops. Make a strip with 144 loops on each side. Insert hook into first 8 loops on second strip, join on yarn and work 1 single crochet.

2 Slip stitch into first center stitch on third strip. Now work 10 chains, insert hook through next 12 loops on third strip and work 1 single crochet.

ork a slip stitch into center single
het between 8th and 9th loops on
nd strip.

4 Work 10 chains, insert hook into next 8 loops on second strip and work 1 single crochet.

5 Slip stitch into center single crochet between 12th and 13th loops on third strip.

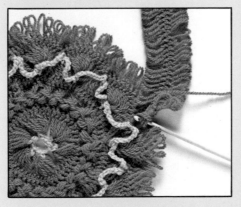

ntinue in this way along strip, then
strip into a circle by joining first and
oops and center stitches.

7 The fourth strip is joined by linking strips. Make a strip with 216 loops on each side. Insert hook into next 2 loops on third strip and next 3 loops on fourth strip, draw the 3 loops of fourth strip through the 2 loops of third strip so having 3 loops on hook. This links the strips together.

8 Insert hook into next 2 loops on third strip and draw them through the 3 loops on hook.

continued

Fred Mancini

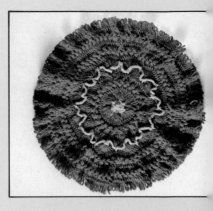

9 Continue to link loops in this way along strip. Join strip into a circle as before.

10 The fifth strip is joined in the same way as the fourth strip. Make a strip with 324 loops on each side. Follow steps 7 and 8, reading fourth strip for third and fifth strip for fourth.

11 Close center as for "Linking strips t form a circle."

Stitch Wise

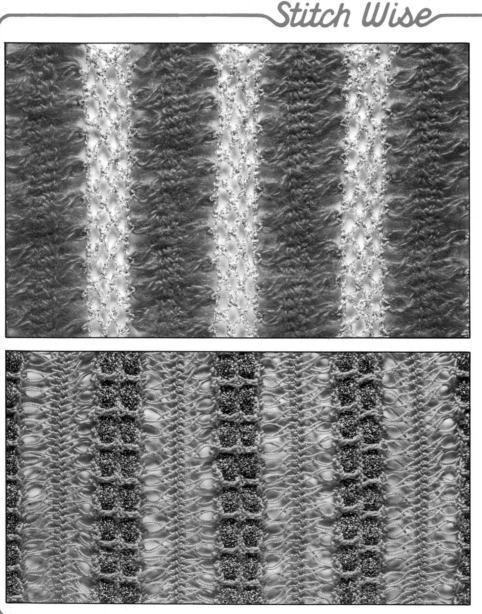

Chain loop joining

Using 1¾in (45mm) hairpin loom, size (5.00mm) hook and mohair-type yarr make strips with a multiple of 3 loops each side.
To edge strips using size E (3.50mm) crochet hook and glitter yarn
1st row Insert crochet hook into first 3 loops and using glitter yarn work 1 sc, *3ch, insert hook into next 3 loops and work 1 sc, rep from * to end of strip. Tu
2nd row *5ch, 1 sc into next loop, rep from * to end, finishing 5ch, sl st into last sc. Fasten off.
To join strips
Join yarn to center of first loop on one strip with a sl st, now sl st into corresponding loop on other strip, *3c sl st into next loop on one strip and corresponding loop on other strip, rep from * to end of strip. Fasten off.

Ribbon-threaded joining

Using a 1½in (40mm) loom, size D (3.25mm) hook and crochet cotton, make strips with a multiple of 2 loops each side.
To edge strips
1st row Insert crochet hook through fi 2 loops, join on yarn and work 1 sc, *2c insert hook through next 2 loops and work 1 sc, rep from * to end of strip. Tu
2nd row 5ch, 1 dc into next sc, *2ch, 1 into next sc, rep from * to end. Fasten Sew strips together, then thread ½in (1cm)-wide ribbon through last row holes on each edging.

cular tablecloth

openwork cloth worked
hairpin lace looks pretty
ed over a plain cloth in a
rdinating color.

Size
Approximately 35½in (90cm) diameter.

Materials
980yd (900m) of a lightweight
  crochet cotton
3¼in (80mm) hairpin loom
Size E (3.50mm) crochet hook

To make
1st strip Using 3¼in (80mm) loom, size
E (3.50mm) hook and working sc at
center, make a strip with 88 loops on
each side.
Insert hook into first 8 loops on one side,
join on yarn and work 1sc, 1ch, *insert
hook into next 8 loops and work 1sc,

1 ch, rep from * to end of strip, sl st into first sc to form a circle. Fasten off.

2nd strip Make a strip with 176 loops on each side. Join 2nd strip to first strip, sl 4 loops from 2nd strip onto hook, sl 2 loops from first strip onto hook and draw them through the 4 loops, sl 4 loops from 2nd strip onto hook and draw them through the 2 loops, cont in this way to end of strip, join to form circle at center st and loops.

3rd strip Work a strip with 264 loops on each side. Sl 8 loops from 2nd strip onto hook, join on yarn and work 1 sc, sl st into first center st of 3rd strip, 10ch, sl 12 loops from 3rd strip onto hook and work 1 sc, sl st between 8th and 9th loops of 2nd strip, 10ch, sl 8 loops of

2nd strip onto hook and work 1 sc, sl st between 12th and 13th loops on 3rd strip, cont in this way to end of strip, join into a circle as before.

4th strip Work a strip with 396 loops on each side. Sl 2 loops from 3rd strip onto hook and 3 loops from 4th strip and draw the 3 loops through the 2 loops, sl 2 loops from 3rd strip onto hook and draw them through the 3 loops, cont in this way to end of strip, join into a circle as before.

5th strip Work a strip with 594 loops on each side. Join as for 3rd and 4th strips.

6th strip Work a strip with 648 loops on each side. Sl 11 loops from 5th strip onto hook and work 1 sc, sl st into first center st of 6th strip, 10ch, sl 12 loops from 6th

strip onto hook and work 1 sc, sl st between 11th and 12th loops on 5th strip, 10ch, sl 11 loops of 5th strip on hook and work 1 sc.

Cont in this way to end of strip, join i a circle as before.

7th strip Work a strip with 972 loops each side.

Join as for 4th to 5th strip.

Edging

*Sl 12 loops onto hook and work 1 sc 10ch, sl st between 12th and 13th lo at center sts *, rep from * to end of str Fasten off.

Center

Join yarn to one chain and work 3 ch 1 dc into each st around center, draw through the top of each dc, gather tig

* Altering garments with
  cable panels
* Where to use cable panels
* Stitch Wise: two-color
  cable patterns
* Pattern for child's sweater
  with cable inserts

ering garments with cable panels

garments with this type of cable l are specifically designed with later tation and alterations in mind. This particularly good idea for children's

clothing, when you consider the cost of the yarn and the amount of time that knitting takes. The cable panel is a completely separate insert instead of

being part of the main fabric. In this way, when you need to enlarge the garment, you can easily unpick the panel and make another, larger one to replace it.

is is a smaller version of the sweater vn on page 32. It has a cable panel e center front and back; also the sleeve orked in two halves with a central e panel that continues to form a saddle ılder.

2 With alteration in mind, the garment is constructed in a slightly unusual way— the waistband and cuffs are knitted on at the end, for ease of undoing. When you need to replace the cable panel, rip out the waistband and cuff seams, then simply unravel the ribbing from the lower, bound-off edge.

3 The next stage is to remove the neckband. As the band comprises stitches picked up from around the neck edge, all you do is rip out the bound-off stitches and unravel the knitting.

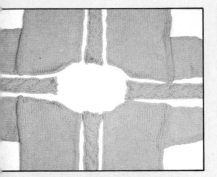

refully rip out all the backstitch ns—first between front and back ions, then between the main sleeve saddle seams. You also need to ove the cable panels so that the nal garment is now in eight pieces.

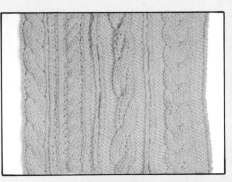

5 To gain extra body width—normally to make the garment one chest size, or 2in (5cm), larger—you must make wider cable panels for the front and back. At left is the original panel; to the right are three alternatives you might use to replace it. The extra panels are all about $1\frac{1}{4}$in (3cm) wider than the original: experiment to determine the number of stitches needed for this extra width. Add the extra stitches in the cable itself or to the border stitches on each side of it.

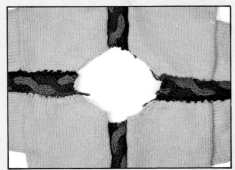

6 The new cable is also inserted in the sleeve to give it extra width. As the cable panel here continues into a saddle shoulder, the width forms part of the neck and makes it bigger. If you do not have any left-over yarn from the original garment, avoid discrepancies in shade by using harmonizing colors in a two-color cable (see Stitch Wise, page 31). Sew the new panels into the appropriate sections.

continued

Mike Berend

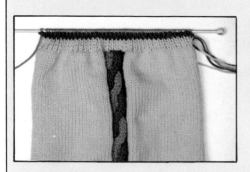

7 In addition to widening the body, you must also lengthen it. The new cable panel across the shoulder already adds ⅝in (1.5cm) to the length. More length –about ¾in (2cm) – can be added in the waistband. Rib to the required depth, adding stripes in the same colors as the new cables.

8 The sleeve can also be lengthened with a deeper cuff, using a stripe sequence that picks out the color of the cables. A wider panel in the center front and back makes the drop shoulder line lower – here it is ⅝in (1.5cm) on each side; this automatically makes the sleeve the same amount lower – or longer.

9 Before joining the main sleeve and s seams to complete the "new" sweater pick up stitches around the neck for th neckband. Be guided by the number c stitches in the original pattern, but allc extra stitches across new cable panels The stripe pattern echoes that of the waistband and cuffs.

Where to use cable panels

It is easiest to replace cable panels in a garment that has existing cables designed especially for alteration. In this case they are usually in the center of a section of knitting so that the pieces on each side are made in the same way.

If you are altering a garment without cables, they most conveniently fit into vertical seams; if you want horizc cables in the middle of a piece of kni you must first divide the fabric Volume 11, pages 49 and 50).

The panels in this jumper cater for a growing child by lengthening and widening the garment. First divide the knitting an appropriate distance above the hem and add a horizontal insertion between the two sections for extra length. Insert a panel in each side seam to widen the garment.

This sweater is specially designed with removable cable panels so that it can easily be adapted at a later stage. The front, back and sleeves are all in two sections so that you can add wider cables for extra width (also adding length in some places). Length is also added in the waistband and cuffs. Two-color cables and stripes add interest and are useful if you do not have any of the original yarn.

The cable panels on this re-styled V-neck sweater are suitable not only for enlarging a growing child's garment but also for giving a new look to an adult's. Divide the fabric above the waistband and use the waistband yarn to lengthen the body. Add cable panels on each side of the front and back in a contrasting color. Pick up stitches along the lower edge and knit a deeper ribbing in the same color as the cables. Work the cuffs in the same way.

Lynn Riding

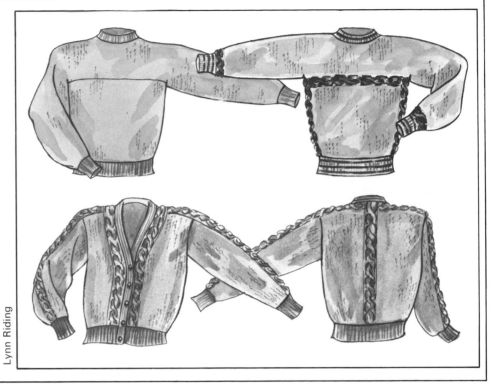

Lynn Riding

riginal garment here is a T-shaped
ter in which the sleeves and yoke are
ed in one, from cuff to cuff. It can be
hened by adding cable panels
e the cuffs and in the body, just
w the armpits. Extra width is gained
serting panels in the side seams, then
ng on a new waistband.

can also design a cardigan with
ing cable panels that can be altered
n necessary—in a way similar to that
for the beige pullover shown
osite. The main pieces are in separate
ons, divided by cables; the cuffs and
tband are worked on stitches picked
om the main sections at the end so
hey can easily be undone.

Stitch Wise

-color cable patterns

-color cables make ideal replacement
ls when altering garments. By
sing two shades harmonizing, or
rasting with the main color, you can
uise any differences in dye lots that
t from buying extra yarn at a later
e. This type of cable requires some
and patience. In addition to the usual
ng techniques, you must also know
t handling two balls of yarn in
red knitting (see Volume 12, pages 57
58).

cables here need small, separate
of color for various sections of
esign; the yarns must be twisted
ther when changing color to prevent
e. It is impossible to strand the
r not in use across the back of the
. If the cable is knitted correctly,
ack side is as neat as the front.

ssic two-color cable

cable requires 2 colors coded as
d B. Before beginning work, check
you have 2 balls in each color or
an extra ball of each.
panel is worked over 12 stitches.
on 6 sts with A, then 6 sts with B.
ow Using A, P2, K4, using B, K4, P2.
row Using B, K2, P4, using A, P4, K2.
6th rows Rep first and 2nd rows twice.
ow Using A, P2, sl next 4 sts in A
cable needle and leave at front of

Mike Berend

work, using B, K4, join 2nd ball of A to
sts on cable needle and K4, join in 2nd
ball of B and P2.
8th row Using B, K2, using A, P4, using
B, P4, using A, K2.
9th row Using A, P2, using B, K4, using
A, K4, using B, P2.
10th-14th rows Rep 6th and 7th rows
twice, then work 6th row again.
15th row Using A, P2, sl next 4 sts in B
onto cable needle and leave at front of
work, using first ball of A, K4 (cut off
2nd ball of A), using original ball of B,
K4 sts from cable needle (cut off 2nd
ball of B), using B, P2.
16th row As 2nd.
These 16 rows form patt. Rep them
throughout.

Triple enclosing cable

This cable required 2 colors coded as
A and B. Before beginning work, either

wind off another small ball of A, or
check that you have 2 balls in that color.
The panel is worked over 16sts. Cast on
6 sts with A, 4 sts with B, then 6 sts
with A.
1st row Using A, P2, K4, using B, K4,
using A, K4, P2.
2nd row Using A, K2, P4, using B, P4,
using A, P4, K2.
3rd-8th rows Rep first and 2nd rows
3 times.
9th row Using A, P2, sl next 4 sts in A
and 4 sts in B (8 sts in all) onto cable
needle and leave at back of work, cut
off ball of B and 2nd ball of A, using first
ball of A, K next 4 sts in A, rejoin B to
next 4 sts in A on cable needle and K4,
rejoin 2nd ball of A to next 4 sts in B on
cable needle and K4, using A, P2.
10th row As 2nd.
11th-16th rows Rep first and 2nd rows
3 times.
These 16 rows form patt. Rep them
throughout.

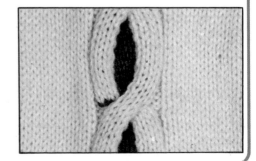

ild's sweater
th cable inserts

front, back and sleeves of
sweater are each made in
pieces so that it's easy to
rt wider cables when the
d grows out of it.

24[26]in (61[66]cm) chest.
th, 14¾(16¼)in (37[41]cm).
ve seam, 11¾[12¾]in (30[33]cm).

Directions for the larger size are
ackets []; if there is only one set of
es it applies to both sizes.

rials
ain sweater 6oz (160g) of a sport
yarn
color cable sweater 6oz (160g)
main color (A)
z (40g) in each of contrasting
colors (B and C)
air each Nos. 3 and 6 (3¼ and
4½mm) needles
ble needle
t of four No. 3 (3¼mm) double-
inted needles

ge
s and 30 rows to 4in (10cm) in
kinette st on No. 6 (4½mm) needles.

half back
g No. 6 (4½mm) needles and main
r, cast on 33 sts. Beg with a K row,
k 11¾in (30cm) stockinette st; end
a P row.
e neck
off 4 sts at beg of next row and
at beg of foll alternate row. Dec one
neck edge on next 5 rows. Work 1
Bind off rem 22 sts.

t half back
k to match left half, reversing neck
ing.

t
k 2 pieces as for back.

t half sleeve
g No. 6 (4½mm) needles and A, cast
3 sts. Beg with a K row, cont in
kinette st, inc one st at beg of 7th and
y foll 6th row until there are 24 sts.
t straight until sleeve measures 10½in
cm); end with a P row. Bind off
ely.

half sleeve
k to match right half, reversing
ing.

e insert (first size back)

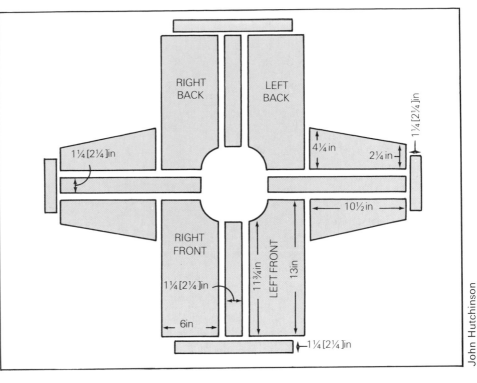

John Hutchinson

RIGHT
BACK

LEFT
BACK

1¼[2¼]in

4¼ in
2¼in

1¼[2¼]in

10½in

RIGHT
FRONT

11¾in
LEFT FRONT
13in

1¼[2¼]in

6in

1¼[2¼]in

Using No. 6 (4½mm) needles and A, cast
on 10 sts.
1st row P2, K6, P2.
2nd row K2, P6, K2.
Rep last 2 rows once more.
5th row P2, sl next 3 sts onto cable
needle and leave at front of work, K3,
then K3 sts from cable needle, P2.
6th row As 2nd.
7th-8th rows As first-2nd.
Rep these 8 rows until work measures
11¾in (30cm); end with a WS row.
Cut off yarn and leave sts on a holder.
Cable insert (second size back)
Cast on 9 sts in B and 9 sts in C.
1st row P3 C, K6 C, K6 B, P3 B.
2nd row K3 B, P6 B, P6 C, K3 C.
Rep last 2 rows twice more.
7th row P3 C, sl next 6 sts onto cable
needle and leave at front of work, K6 B,
join in a 2nd ball of C and K6 sts from
cable needle, join in a 2nd ball of B and
P3 B.
8th row K3 B, P6 C, P6 B, K3 C.
Work 10 more rows as set.
19th row P3 C, sl next 6 sts onto cable
needle and leave at front of work, K6 C,
then K6 sts from cable needle in B, P3 B,
breaking off 2nd ball of each color.
20th row As 2nd.
21st-24th rows Rep first-2nd rows twice.
Rep these 24 rows until work measures
11¾in (30cm); end with a WS row.
Cut off yarn and leave sts on a holder.
Both sizes
Make another piece in the same way for
the front, then 2 pieces, each 14½in (37cm)
long for the sleeves.

Waistband
Sew cable insert between 2 halves of
back. Using No. 3 (3¼mm) needles, A

and with RS facing, pick up and K 33 sts
along lower edge of first half, 9[15] sts
across cable and 33 sts along 2nd half.
75[81] sts.
1st size only
Work 1¼in (3cm) K1, P1 ribbing. Bind
off loosely.
2nd size only
Work in K1, P1 ribbing in stripe sequence
of 3 rows A, 2 rows B, 2 rows C, 4 rows
A, 2 rows C, 2 rows B and 3 rows A.
Bind off loosely in A. Assemble front and
complete waistband in same way.

Cuffs
Sew cable insert between 2 halves of
sleeve, with top 4in (10cm) forming
saddle shoulder. Using No. 3 (3¼mm)
needles, A and with RS facing, pick up
and K 13 sts across first half, 9[15] sts
across cable, then 13 sts across 2nd half.
35[41] sts. Rib as for waistband.

Neckband
Sew saddle shoulder sections of cables
into shoulder seams. Using set of four
No. 3 (3¼mm) needles, A and with RS
facing, pick up and K 11 sts along each
shaped edge of neck and 7[11] sts
across each cable. 80[96] sts.
1st size only
Work 1¼in (3cm) in rounds of K1, P1
ribbing.
Bind off loosely.
2nd size only
Work in rounds of K1, P1 ribbing in stripe
sequence of 3 rounds A, 2 each in B and
C, then 3 rounds in A. Bind off loosely in A.

To finish
Press or block according to yarn used.
Join side and sleeve seams. Press seams.

*Filet lace knitting
*Filet lace insertions
*Pattern for a woman's cardigan with filet lace panel

Filet lace knitting

This is a type of knitting—used mainly for insertions and edgings—that closely resembles the popular, lacy-look filet crochet work. As in the crochet version, a square mesh background is filled with a pattern comprising blocks and spaces. The lace is worked in garter stitch. Each block consists of three stitches and is four rows deep. A space is also worked over three stitches, but is only two rows deep; so in order to work a complete space, to balance a block, you must work one space on top of another. The two are separated by a narrow bar of knitting.

Sample of filet lace knitting.

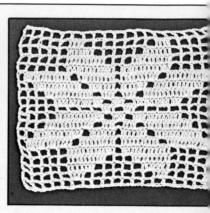

Sample of filet crochet.

Working a space

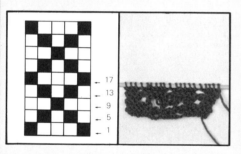

1 Filet lace patterns are clearest when shown in their chart form of blocks and spaces. Here the design consists of 5 blocks/spaces across the width. The sample shows 2 complete lines (8 rows of pattern), including three edge stitches at each side.

2 To make a space you need 3 stitches. Here the space is the first one in the 3rd line (9th row). After 3 edge stitches have been worked, bring the yarn forward between the needles, then over the top of right-hand needle to the back and around to the front between the needles again.

3 Slip the next stitch on the left-hand needle knitwise, then also slip the following stitch in the same way. Use left-hand needle point to lift the first slipped stitch over the second and off right-hand needle, so binding off one stitch.

4 Slip a third stitch onto right-hand needle and bind off another stitch by lifting the second slipped stitch over the third. Return remaining loop to left-hand needle and knit it. You now have 3 loops on the right-hand needle (plus the edge stitches). To make an adjacent space, as on chart, repeat steps 2 through 4.

5 The following (wrong-side) row of a block and space pattern is always worked in the same way. Each stitch is knitted except the second "made" stitch of a space (the center stitch), which must be purled. The 2 adjacent spaces are clearly visible here.

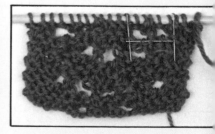

6 To square the space worked over the last 2 rows, you must repeat these row again. The 2 adjacent spaces worked o the last 4 rows are marked here with pins; the horizontal pin marks the cross bar that divides any complete space in filet knitting.

rking a block

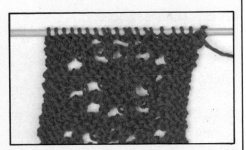

e 4th line of pattern shown in step "Working a space" requires a space, a block to be made. Simply knit the tches at the postion of the block. e you can see that the 3 stitches are ediately over a space in the previous of pattern.

2 As the background fabric of filet lace is basically garter stitch, 4 rows must be worked to make a square block. The block stitches are knitted on every row. The block described in step 1 is shown here after it has been completed in the 16th row.

3 When a block changes to a space (as it does in the 2nd square of the 5th line of pattern shown in step 1 of "Working a space"), simply use the 3 stitches knitted to form a block for working the space movements described in steps 2 to 4, page 34. Here the 5th line is complete.

et lace insertions

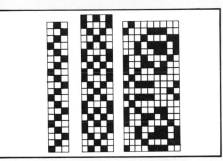

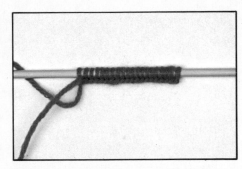

ric made in filet lace knitting is usually lacy and open to wear without some of lining. However, strips of filet lace erns make ideal insertions between pieces of fabric in the same way as nary lace is used in dressmaking.

1 The width of an insertion varies according to the yarn you are using and the number of blocks and spaces in a line of pattern. A strip 3 squares wide makes a narrow border with room for only a simple pattern, while between 7 to 9 squares make a much wider border with more scope for designs. Make up your own patterns on charts as shown, or use existing crochet or embroidery designs.

2 Once you know the techniques of making blocks and spaces you can knit your own designs from a chart. Calculate the number of stitches to cast on by the number of stitches in one line of the chart. Allow 3 stitches for each square plus 5 extra edge stitches (3 for one edge, 2 for the other). Therefore, the design shown below requires 20 cast-on stitches.

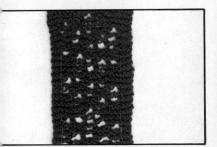

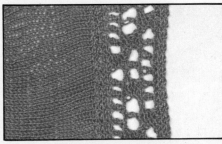

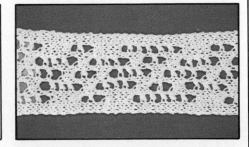

t the beginning of each row, before rking any block or space stitches, knit rder stitches. Knit 2 border stitches at end of each row: only 2 stitches are essary as the last stitch of the pattern ances the number. The border makes at, straight edge to the insertion; it so useful when sewing the lace in ition.

If you use this insertion on the edge of a fabric—see the cardigàn on page 36—the edge stitches automatically form the outer border such as the button or buttonhole band.
The insertion is knitted separately and then joined to the main fabric with an ordinary backstitch seam on the wrong side of the work.

A lacy insertion is a simple way of trimming a fabric tablecloth, tray cloth or napkin. Here filet lace is used as an overlay on top of a solid-colored fabric. When the lace is sewn in place, the background color shows through the spaces. Sew the panel in position neatly using a matching thread.

Mike Berend

Cardigan with filet lace panel

This mint-cool short-sleeved cotton cardigan, edged with knitted filet lace, will dress up your slimline separates.

32[34:36:38]in (83[87:92:97]
bust.
th, 23½[24:24½:24¾]in (59[60:61:
m).

Directions for the larger sizes are
ckets [ ]; if there is only one set of
es it applies to all sizes.

erials
pprox 15[15:17:19]oz (400[400:
450:500]g) of a medium-weight
mercerized crochet cotton
pair each Nos. 2 and 3 (2¾ and
3¼mm) needles
buttons

je
s and 32 rows to 4in (10cm) in
inette st on No. 3 (3¼mm) needles.

Back

Using No. 2 (2¾mm) needles cast on
103[109:115:121] sts.
1st row K1, *P1, K1, rep from * to end.
2nd row P1, *K1, P1, rep from * to end.
Rep last 2 rows for 2in (5cm); end with a
2nd row.
Change to No. 3 (3¼mm) needles. Beg
with a K row, cont in stockinette st until
work measures 12in (30cm); end with
a P row.

Shape sleeves

Inc 1 st at each end of next and every
foll 4th row until there are
119[125:131:137] sts, then at each end
of every other row until there are
143[149:155:161] sts; end with a P row.
Cast on 4 sts at beg of next 6 rows.
167[173:179:185] sts.
Cont straight for 5½[6:6¼:6¾]in
(14[15:16:17]cm); end with a P row.
Bind off loosely.

Left front

Using No. 2 (2¾mm) needles cast on
51[55:57:61] sts. Rib 2in (5cm) as for
back, ending with a 2nd row and inc one
st at end of last row on first and 3rd
sizes only. 52[55:58:61] sts.
Change to No. 3 (3¼mm) needles.
Next row K31[34:37:40], K twice into
next st, turn and leave rem 20 sts on a
holder.
Cont in stockinette st until work measures
12in (30cm); end with a P row.

Shape sleeves and front edge

Inc 1 st at beg (side edge) of next and
every foll 4th row 8 times in all, every other
row 12 times, then cast on 4 sts 3 times,
at same time shape front edge by working

"K to last 3 sts, sl 1, K1, psso" on next and
every foll 4th row 20[21:22:23] times
in all. 45[47:49:51] sts.
Cont straight until work measures same
as back to shoulder; end with a P row.
Bind off loosely. Using No. 3 (3¼mm)
needles and with RS facing, rejoin yarn
to 20 sts for filet lace panel.
1st row K3, (yo twice to make 2 sts, sl 2,
pass first slipped st over 2nd, sl another st,
then pass first st over this again, sl rem
st back onto left-hand needle and K it—
called space "sp") twice, K3 sts—called
block "blk"—, 2 sps, K2.
2nd and every other row K to end, working
(K1, P1) into 2 made sts.
3rd row As first.
5th and 7th rows K3, 1 sp, 1 blk, 1 sp,
1 blk, 1 sp, K2.
9th and 11th rows K3, 1 blk, 3 sps, 1 blk,
K2.
13th and 15th rows As 5th and 7th rows.
17th and 19th rows As first.
20th row As 2nd. Rep these 20 rows until
work is same length as edge of front; end
with a WS row.
Next row Bind off 17, K to end.
Work in garter st on these 3 sts to center
back neck. Bind off.

Right front

Using No. 2 (2¾mm) needles cast on
51[55:57:61]sts. Rib 2in (5cm) as
for back; end with a 2nd row and inc
1 st at beg of last row on first and 3rd
sizes only. 52[55:58:61] sts.
Change to No. 3 (3¼mm) needles.
Next row K3, work 2 sps, 1 blk, 2 sps, K2,
turn and leave rem sts on a holder. Cont on
these sts to match left front; end with a
RS row.
Next row Bind off 17, K to end.
Work in garter st on 3 sts to center back
neck. Bind off.
Using No. 3 (3¼mm) needles and with
RS facing, rejoin yarn to rem sts, K
twice into first st, K to end. Complete to
match left front, reversing shaping.

Sleeve panel

Using No. 3 (3¼mm) needles cast on
20 sts loosely. Work 11[12:12½:13½]in
(28[30:32:34]cm) patt as for front filet
lace panel. Bind off.

Cuff

Using No. 2 (2¾mm) needles and with
RS facing, pick up and K 57[61:65:69]
sts along one edge of panel (right-hand
edge for left sleeve and left-hand edge
for right sleeve). Rib 2in (5cm) as for
back. Bind off loosely in ribbing.

To finish

Press or block according to yarn used. Sew
front panels to front edges. Join shoulder
seams. Sew garter st border to back, joining
at center back. Sew sleeve panels to
sleeves. Join side and underarm seams;
press. Sew 5 buttons to left front
and make loops to correspond.

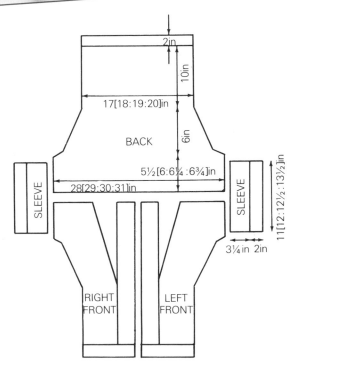

*Filet lace edging
*Designing filet lace
  edgings and insertions
*Stitch Wise: unusual filet
  lace edgings and insertions
*Pattern for a cradle canopy
  cover

Filet lace edging

Filet lace knitting comprises block and space patterns on a mesh background (see pages 34 and 35 for the basic techniques of working blocks and spaces).
Filet lace edgings have one straight edge for sewing onto the fabric; the other edge is shaped according to the pattern. The shaping consists of increasing or decreasing blocks or spaces. However, preparations are made for these increases and decreases in the rows immediately preceding them. Details of how to work an edging from a chart are shown here.

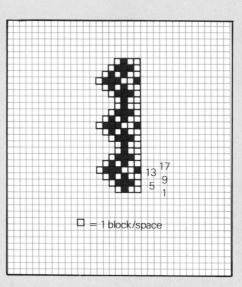

13 17
5   9
     1

□ = 1 block/space

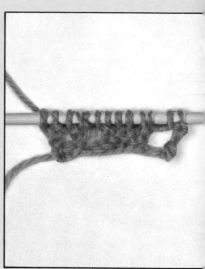

1 The edging is usually worked from a chart like the one shown above.
Calculate the stitches to cast on from the number of blocks and spaces in the first line—here there are 4. Each block or space requires 3 stitches. Allow 1 extra stitch for a neat border at the right-hand edge, making 13 stitches in all.

2 Cast on the required number of stitch and, keeping a border of 1 knit stitch a the right-hand edge, work 2 rows in pattern (2 spaces, 1 block and 1 space described in "Filet lace knitting," page and 35: The photograph shows the wo with the first 2 rows completed and th edge to be shaped at right.

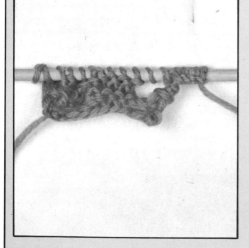

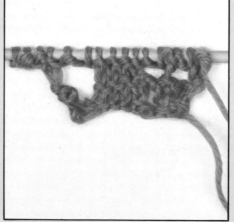

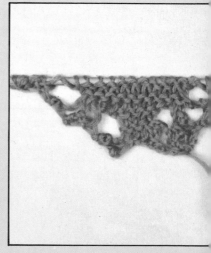

3 The 5th row requires 3 extra stitches at the left-hand edge (to make a space). Provision for this increase must be made at the end of the 3rd row. Work the 3rd row in the pattern as usual, then turn the work and cast on 3 stitches.

4 Work the next row in the usual way including knitting the extra stitches. One line of pattern is now complete. Note the base for the new space in the 2nd line at the left-hand edge.

5 Continue to work the 2nd line (rows 5 to 8) in pattern from the chart. At the end of the 7th row cast on 3 more stitches for the extra space at the left-hand edge of the 3rd line.

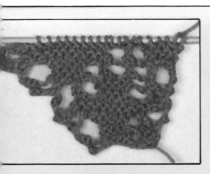

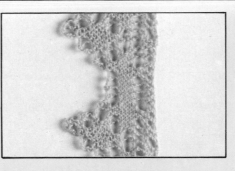

...epare for a decrease by binding off 3 ...hes (or the correct multiple of ...hes) at the beginning of the wrong-...row (here it is the 16th) immediately ...re starting the line in which the ...k/space is decreased.

7 Continue in pattern from the chart, increasing and decreasing at the left-hand edge as required. Here you can see the delicate effect of the pattern when it is worked in a cotton yarn.

8 Although it is worked widthwise, with shaping at the left-hand edge, the finished edging usually hangs downward with the shaping at the lower edge. Place the 1-stitch border along the edge to to be trimmed and sew it in place.

...signing filet lace edgings and insertions

...e you have mastered the techniques ...aking a mesh background, it is easy ...ock in squares to make a pattern. ...most filet lace fabrics are simple ...es, usually for insertions and edg-..., there is no need to work out com-...ted instructions. A simple chart gives ...ear visual guide to working; it is easy ...evise a chart to your own specifica-...s.

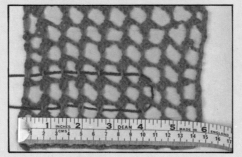

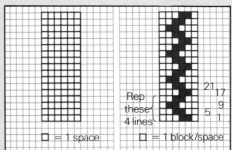

1 Using the appropriate yarn and needles, make a plain mesh (see "Working a space," page 34) to use as a guide to the number of squares you can have in each line of pattern. Cast on multiples of 3 stitches plus an extra edge stitch and experiment until you have a mesh about 4in (10cm) square. Here 6 squares measure 4in (10cm) across the width.

2 Find—or make up—a suitable design. Remember that if your insertion is to be 4in (10cm) wide, you are restricted to 6 blocks or spaces across a line. The easiest way to make a chart is to draw a grid on graph paper as shown at left above. Block in the pattern as desired.

□ = 1 space   □ = 1 block/space

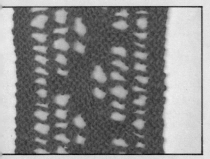

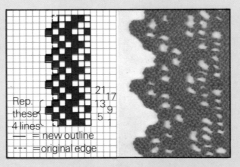

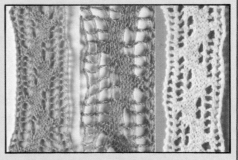

...orking directly from the chart, cast ...he required number of stitches—6 ...ks/spaces × 3=18. You also require ...e stitches for a neat border (3 at the ...nning of rows and 2 at the end for an ...rtion): that makes a total of 23 ...hes. Also note that you must work 4 ...s in pattern to complete one line of ...ks and spaces. There is no need to ...w the entire length you are working; ...ly repeat the 4 lines of pattern.

4 Transform an insertion into an edging by increasing and decreasing blocks or spaces at the left-hand edge to create a serrated finish. The right-hand edge remains straight for sewing onto the fabric. Here the strip in step 2 has been converted into an edging. The last space of each line of pattern at the left-hand edge is blocked in to make the edging hang better. Extra blocks balance the original pattern.

— = new outline
---- = original edge

5 If you have a favorite chart for a block and space pattern, it is interesting to experiment with a variety of yarns or needles for different effects. At left is an insertion in fine crochet cotton knitted on the appropriate needles. In the center, the same yarn has been worked on large needles for an extra-lacy look. At right is an example of the fine work that can be achieved in soft yarns, especially sport yarn qualities.

Mike Berend

Stitch Wise

A variety of filet lace edgings and insertions

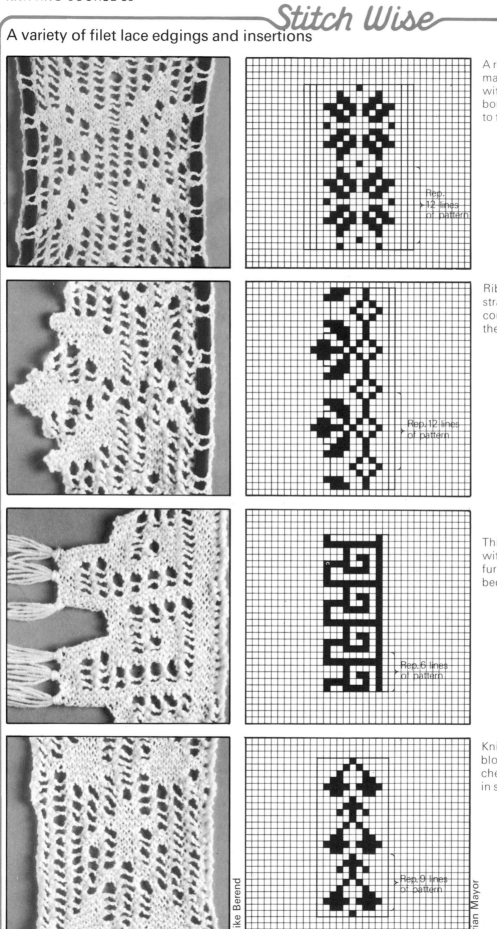

A row of spaces in a filet lace pattern make perfect eyelet holes for threading with ribbon. In this example a 1-space border is left on each edge of this insert to thread the ribbon through.

Rep. 12 lines of pattern

Ribbon is also used to decorate the straight side of this edging (left). You could also use the ribbon for gathering the filet lace for use as a collar or cuff.

Rep. 12 lines of pattern

This geometric-patterned edging finish with tassels (left) is an ideal trim for h furnishings such as window shades, bedspreads and tablecloths.

Rep. 6 lines of pattern

Knit a cherry-patterned insertion in blocks and spaces. The shapes of the cherries and their stalks could be outli in simple, colorful embroidery stitches

Rep. 9 lines of pattern

Mike Berend

Brian Mayor

dle canopy and cover

ome a new baby with a pretty crib blanket and canopy
d with ribbon and delicate knitting.

Sizes

Blanket $26\frac{3}{4} \times 18$in (68×46cm).
Canopy $56\frac{3}{4} \times 37\frac{3}{4}$ (144×96cm).

Materials

$2\frac{3}{4}$yd (2.5m) of 36in (90cm)-wide
  gingham fabric
1 piece of batting $18 \times 23\frac{1}{2}$in
  (46×60cm)
$4\frac{1}{2}$yd (4m) of $\frac{1}{4}$in (5mm)-wide satin
  ribbon
$2\frac{3}{4}$yd (2.5m) of $\frac{3}{4}$in (2cm)-wide
  satin ribbon
490yd (450m) of a medium-weight
  crochet cotton
1 pair No. 3 (3mm) knitting needles

Gauge

Depth of edging at widest point, $3\frac{1}{4}$in
(8cm) worked on No. 3 ($3\frac{1}{4}$mm) needles.

Blanket

Using No. 3 ($3\frac{1}{4}$mm) needles cast on 11 sts.
1st row K2, work 1 sp, 1 blk, 1sp.
2nd and every other row K to end, working
(K1, P1) into the 2 made sts.
3rd row As first row, turn and cast on 6 sts.
5th row K2, work 1 sp, 1 blk, 3 sps.
7th row As 5th row, turn and cast on 3 sts.

9th row K2, work 1 sp, 1 blk, 1sp,
1 blk, 2 sps.
11th row As 9th.
13th and 15th rows K2, work 1 sp,
4 blks, 1 sp.
17th and 19th rows As 9th.
20th row Bind off 3, work to end as
2nd row.
21st and 23rd rows As 5th.
24th row Bind off 6, work to end as
2nd row.
25th and 27th rows As first.
28th row As 2nd.
These 28 rows form patt.
Rep patt rows 9 times more.
Press work on the WS lightly, using a
warm iron over a damp cloth.

To finish

Cut out blanket fabric to measure
$37 \times 24\frac{1}{2}$in (94×62cm). Fold fabric in half
widthwise and stitch down one short
side and long side taking $\frac{3}{8}$in (1cm) seam.
Turn RS out and press. Cut narrow ribbon
to length of edging, plus 4in (10cm).
Thread ribbon through holes close to
straight edge, skipping every 2nd hole
on WS. Turn ends of ribbon under to
WS and stitch. Sew edging to stitched
short edge of cover, overlapping edging

by $\frac{3}{4}$in (2cm). Slip batting inside cov[...]
turn under $\frac{3}{8}$in (1cm) along raw edge[...]
slip stitch in place. Using wide ribbo[...]
make a bow and sew it to center of
edging.

Canopy

Make two lengths of edging, each wi[...]
patts for side edges and a length of
edging with 20 patts for lower edge.
Press lightly, using a warm iron over a[...]
damp cloth.
Using selvages for top and lower edg[...]
canopy, cut out a piece of fabric
$52\frac{3}{4} \times 35\frac{1}{2}$in ($134 \times 90$cm). Turn unde[...]
raw edges $\frac{3}{8}$in (1cm) and stitch to fin[...]
them. Stitch side pieces of lace edgin[...]
to each end of piece made for lower e[...]
Thread narrow ribbon through edging
before. Sew edging to canopy down [...]
and along lower edge.
Fold canopy in half widthwise. With F[...]
together, stitch two rows 1in (2.5cm) [...]
2in (5cm) below top edge for form ca[...]
for rod. Stitch to within $\frac{3}{8}$in (2cm) of
foldline. Turn to RS. Cut remaining w[...]
ribbon into four equal lengths. Make [...]
bows and sew one to each side at top [...]
and one to each bottom front corner.

*Embroidery on knitting
*Satin stitch
*Stem stitch outlining
*Bullion knots on openwork
*Blanket stitch on eyelets
*Stitch Wise: fur stitch
 patterns
*Pattern for a teenager's
 embroidered sweater

broidery on knitting

such a variety of textured and multi-
ed knitted fabrics at our fingertips
rdly seems necessary to use em-
dery on knitting. But embroidery
have one big advantage in that it
be applied to your work as an after-
ght. It is the perfect solution for a
nent—old or new—that needs either
plete revamping or just a little en-

livening with a few subtle highlights.
The embroidery technique most com-
monly applied to knitting is duplicate
stitch—also called Swiss darning—(see
Volume 2, page 38); the stitches follow the
path of the knitted loops. When well
executed, duplicate stitch is almost indis-
tinguishable from Fair Isle knitting.
In this issue you can learn how to add

other embroidery stitches to a plain
stockinette stitch ground or even to openwork, embossed or jacquard fabrics.
When choosing the yarns that you are
going to use, keep in mind that it is not
possible to make fine delicate stitches on
knitting. Use a yarn that is similar in
weight to that of the background and
stay away from very fine threads.

in stitch

re beginning to work satin stitch on
rment, bear in mind that this is not
asiest technique to work on knitting.
following hints should help to
re success. First, because the stitches

will tend to pull the knitting out of shape,
you should baste the fabric to a piece of
stiff paper. Second, never work very long
stitches, or they will be caught and pulled
out with wear. To prevent this, break up a

large area into sections and fill in the
sections separately. Last, always use a
tapestry needle for all embroidery on
knitting to avoid splitting the strands of
yarn.

in stitch lettering

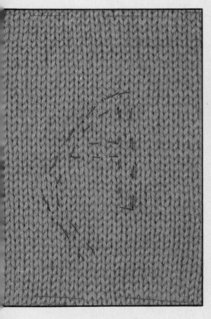

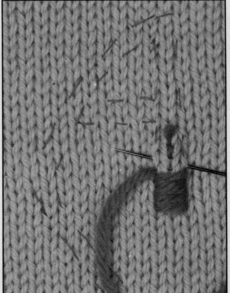

tials are ideal for satin stitch because
can be worked with short, secure
nds. First, baste the area to be worked
a stiff piece of paper, using a
p needle and sewing thread.
n baste the desired shape in place,
g the sewing thread.

2 Fasten the yarn to the knitting with a
couple of backstitches inside the letter.
To fill in the shape, make close, even
stitches, covering the basted outline and
working through the fabric only.

3 When the satin stitching is completed,
fasten off the yarn by passing the needle
back through the stitches and then
cutting the loose end. Remove the paper
and press the fabric face down, using the
method appropriate for the yarn.

Mike Berend

Satin stitch on embossed knitting

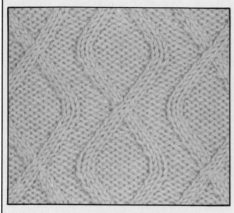

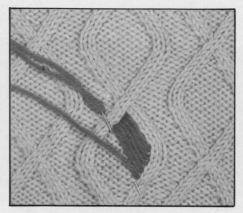

1 The recesses on embossed knitting are a perfect location for satin stitch highlights. Above is an open cable on a reverse stockinette stitch background. When filling such small areas there is no need to baste the knitting to paper.

2 Fasten the yarn to the knitting as explained in step 2 of "satin stitch lettering." Fill in each of the diamond-shaped gaps between the two arms of the cable.

3 These simple fillings change the ent appearance of the knitting fabric by enlivening it with color and adding a contrasting texture.

Stem stitch outlining

Shapes in jacquard knitting will not stand out distinctly if the colors are too similar in tone. To enhance a pattern, try outlining it with stem stitch, using a contrasting tone either lighter or darker than the background colors.

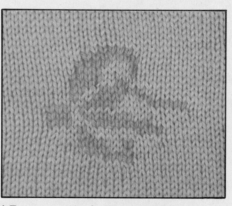

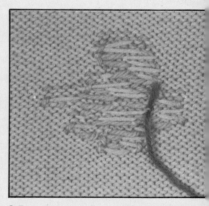

1 To prevent the flower shape from fading into insignificance, choose a color that will stand out suitably as an outline.

2 Fasten the yarn to the back of the w with a few overcasting stitches into th same place. Never use a knot, as it wil pull through to the right side with wea

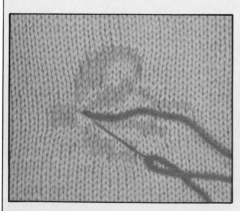

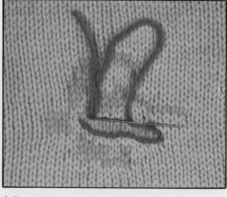

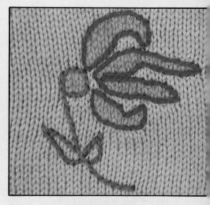

3 Draw the needle through to the front of the work at the outline edge. Insert the needle a short distance from starting point; make a backstitch half that length.

4 Repeat, bringing needle out at the end of previous stitch. Take shorter stitches around sharp curves. When work is complete, fasten off yarn at back.

5 You can work other details, like the stem and leaves above, in different contrasting colors.

on knots on openwork

e past bullion knots were often
d to cotton knitted lace to make it
ser imitation of needle lace. The
will not pull and distort your
ng, as satin stitch tends to do, so
is no need to baste the knitting to a
backing. Use a slightly finer yarn
that of the background. A strand of
n yarn or a few strands of silk or
embroidery floss are suitable.
sample the knots form a cloverleaf
, but the basic technique applies to
ape you may choose.

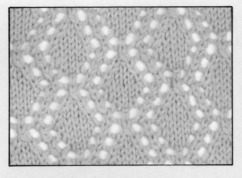

1 Any number of openwork stitch patterns
make a good base for bullion knots. You
need not cover the fabric with knots
but could work them along borders,
cuffs or necklines.

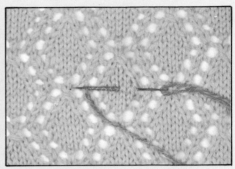

2 Fasten the yarn at the back and
draw the needle through at the center
of the projected clover shape. Insert the
needle a short distance from the center
and bring the point out again at the
center. Before drawing the needle
through, wrap the yarn several times
around the point of the needle.

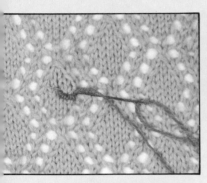

d the wrapped threads between
b and index finger of the left hand
ush the needle through. Then insert
eedle in the same place and draw it
t the center. Make another knot in
ame place as the first.

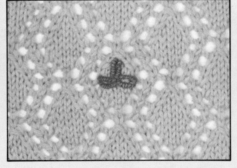

4 Make the other two arms of the clover
in the same way, each with two bullion
knots side by side. The knot will bow if
you have made enough wrappings and
if the strand passing through it is not
too tight.

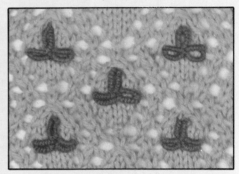

5 After each clover shape is complete,
fasten off the yarn at the back with a
few backstitches. Then begin the next
clover, following steps 2 to 4.

nket stitch on eyelets

her way of highlighting openwork
ng is by decorating the eyelet holes.
ugh it is possible to use a simple
casting stitch around the eyelets,
ket stitch will make a more even
ng. Use a yarn that is slightly finer
the one used for the background.

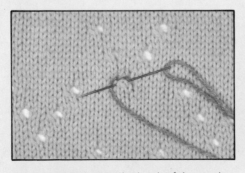

1 Fasten the yarn to the back of the work
and draw the needle through about $\frac{1}{8}$in
(3mm) from the edge of the eyelet. Pass
the needle through the center of the eyelet
and out a little to the left of the starting
point and over the working yarn. The
stitch can also be worked in the opposite
way, with the loops at the center.

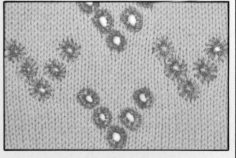

2 Continue making stitches closely all
around the eyelet. Work each eyelet in
the same way. Eyelets sprinkled over a
stockinette stitch fabric and edged with a
contrasting color in this way produce a
lovely lacy effect.

Mike Berend

Stitch Wise

Fur stitch

Cast on odd numbers of sts.
1st row (WS) K.
2nd row K1, *K1 but do not let st drop off left-hand needle, yarn to front, pass yarn over thumb of left hand to make a loop, yarn to back and K same st again letting st drop off left-hand needle in usual way, yarn to front, then back over needle to form a loop, pass 2 sts just worked over this loop—called loop 1 —, K1, rep from * to end.
3rd row K.
4th row K2, *loop 1, K1, rep from * to last st, K1.
These 4 rows form patt.

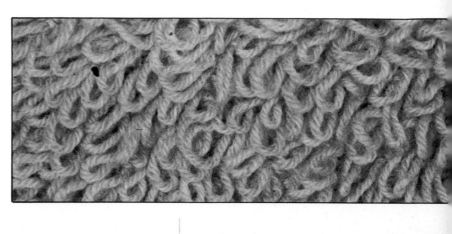

Ladder fur stitch

Cast on an even number of stitches.
1st-6th rows K.
7th row *K1, (yo) 4 times, rep from * to last st, K1.
8th row K to end, dropping the extra loops and drawing out the sts.
3rd-8th rows form the patt.
"Fur" Take two 4in (10cm) lengths of yarn. Insert a crochet hook under 4 long sts, fold strands of yarn in half, place loop on hook and draw hook through, so drawing loops through. Now draw ends of yarn through loop on hook. Make a knot into every 4 long sts.

Mike Berend

Teenager's embroidered sweater

Highlight a pretty sweater with embroidery and go to the top of the class.

Sizes

To fit 32[34:36:38]in (83[87:92:97] cm) bust.
Length, 20½[21:21¼:21¾]in (52[53:54:55]cm).
Sleeve seam, 6in (15cm).

Note Directions for the larger sizes are in brackets []; if there is only one set of figures it applies to all sizes.

Materials

6[8:8:10]oz (150[200:200:250]g) of a sport yarn for sweater
Leftover lengths of 2 shades of pink and some green yarn for embroidery
1 pair each Nos. 2 and 3 (2¾ and 3¼mm) knitting needles

Gauge

28 sts and 36 rows to 4in (10cm) in stockinette st on No. 3 (3¼mm) needles.

Back

**Using No. 2 (2¾mm) needles cast on 109[115:123:129] sts.
1st row K2, *P1, K1, rep from * to last st, K1.
2nd row *K1, P1, rep from * to last st, K1. Rep last 2 rows for 3½in (9cm); end with a 2nd row. Change to No. 3 (3¼mm) needles.
Next row K8[11:8:11], K into front and back of next st, *K12[12:14:14], K into front and back of next st, rep from * to last 9[12:9:12] sts, K to end. 117[123:131:137] sts.
Beg with a P row, work 15 rows stockinette st.
Beg patt.
1st row K4[7:11:14], *yo, K2 tog, K25, rep from * ending with K3[6:10:13] instead of K25.
2nd to 34th rows Beg with a P row, work in stockinette st.
These 34 rows form patt. Patt 30 more rows. Place a marker at each end of last row to denote beg of armholes. **
Shape raglan armholes
Cont to work eyelets above those already made on every 34th row, and at the same time dec one st at each end of every row until 111[113:117:119] sts rem, then at each end of every other row until 41[41:43:43] sts rem. Work 1 row. Bind off loosely.

Front

Work as given for back from ** to **.
Shape raglan armholes
Cont to work in patt as for back, and a[t] same time dec one st at each end of ev[ery] row until 111[113:117:119] sts rem, then at each end of every other row un[til] 57[57:59:59] sts rem.
Shape neck
Next row P21, bind off 15[15:17:17] loosely, P to end.
Cont on last set of sts. Dec at armhole edge on next and foll alternate rows, a[t] **same time** dec one st at neck edge on next 6 rows, then 5 foll alternate rows[.] K2 tog.
Fasten off. With RS facing, rejoin yarn[.] rem sts at neck edge and complete to match first side.

Sleeves

Using No. 2 (2¾mm) needles cast on 73[75:77:79] sts. Rib 10 rows as for back waistband. Change to No. 3 (3¼[mm] needles. Beg with a K row, work 4 row[s] stockinette st. Cont in stockinette st, i[nc] one st at each end of next and foll 6th row. Work 3 rows. Beg patt.
1st row K11[12:13:14], *yo, K2 tog, K25, rep from * once more, yo, K2 tog[,] K to end.
Cont in patt as set, work 1 row. Inc on[e] st at each end of next and every foll 6t[h]

row until there are 85[87:89:91] sts.
Work 9 more rows. Place a marker at each
end of last row to denote beg of sleeve
top. Work another 4[6:8:10] rows.
Shape top
Dec one st at each end of next and every
foll alternate row until 15 sts rem. Work 1
row.
Bind off loosely.

Neckband
Join front and right back raglan seams.

Using No. 2 (2¾mm) needles and with
RS facing, pick up and K 16 sts along left
sleeve top, 19 sts down left side of front,
15[15:17:17] sts across bound off sts,
19 sts up right side of neck, 15 sts along
right sleeve top and 45[45:47:47] sts
along back neck.
1st row *K1, P1, rep from * to last st, K1.
2nd row K2, *P1, K1, rep from * to last
st, K1.
Rep last 2 rows 7 times more. Bind off
loosely in ribbing.

To finish
Do not press. Join left back raglan an
neckband seams.
Fold neckband in half to WS and slip
stitch in place. Embroider as shown,
selecting eyelet holes as desired. Usi
one shade of pink, work 8 petals into
eyelet hole with lazy stitch (see Volur
18, page 76). Blanket stitch around h
using another shade of pink. Using gr
work stems in stem stitch and leaves i
bullion knots. Join side and sleeve se

Shoestring

Westward ho!

Bright, contrasting fringe adds a flavor of the Old West to a plain jumpsuit. Or, if you prefer, trim the seams with braid.

Materials
Jumpsuit
Purchased fringe ¾-2in (2-5cm)
deep (for amount see step 2);
or ¾-1in (2-2.5cm)-wide braid
Matching thread

Decide which seams on the garment lend themselves to trimming. Yokes, seams, collars and pocket flaps are ally the best lines to accentuate.

2 Estimate the amount of fringe or braid you will need: measure each seam accurately and add 2in (5cm) for turning under 1in (2.5cm) at each end. Add up the separate amounts for each seam to get the total required. Remember that if the garment is to be washed, the fringe or braid must also be washable. Buy a little extra in this case, and wash it (and the jumpsuit, if new) before sewing the fringe or braid in place.

3 Cut the required length of fringe for each seam, allowing extra for turning under as explained above.
4 Pin and baste the fringe along each of the seam lines, first turning under the ends of the fringe.
5 Hand-sew the fringe in place, using matching thread and backstitch. If you are using braid, place the upper edge along the seamline and sew it in place, leaving the other edge free.

*Cutting and finishing
sequined fabrics
*Making a strapless top
of sequined fabric
*Pattern for a coat and
eight-gore skirt (1):
adapting the pattern

Cutting and finishing sequined fabrics

Sequined fabrics may be heavily encrusted or only sprinkled lightly with sequins. In either case it is advisable to choose a garment with very few seams and dartings, such as a shapeless top, or "boob tube."

Non-stretch sequined fabrics can be sequined all over or have sequined motifs applied at intervals. The methods of joining are the same for stretch and non-stretch fabrics, except that it is advisable to use a stretch stitch when assembling stretch fabrics.

1 When cutting out the pattern pieces, lay them on the right side of the fabric so that they lie in the same direction. This is especially important if the sequins are overlapped in one direction. Match up any motifs included in the material.

2 Pin within the seam allowance and to avoid cutting sequins. Cut each pi[ece] separately.

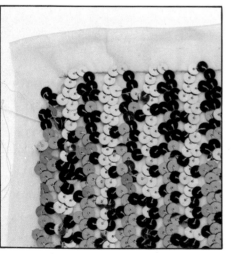

3 If the sequins are close together, remove the appropriate number from within the seam allowance using small scissors before cutting the fabric. Then fasten the sequin threads to prevent the remainder of the sequins from falling off. Re-apply sequins to cover gaps, when all seaming is complete.

4 When stitching, use a zipper foot. Remove sequins from the hem and seam allowances. Use snaps and hooks and eyes instead of buttons and zippers wherever possible.

5 When pressing, use a cool, dry iron. Press on the wrong side with a dry press cloth over a padded board.

Simon Butcher

king a strapless top of sequined fabric

ob tubes'' are fun and easy to make
stretch fabric of the correct width.
have made one of sequined stretch
c, but the same principles can be
ied to any stretch fabric.
make a sequined boob tube, buy a
th of stretch sequined fabric and
together the two ends using the
nod described here. Estimated lengths
yd (.7m) for size 10; ⅞yd (.8m) for
12 and 14; 1yd (.9m) for sizes 16
18; 1⅛yd (1m) for size 20. These
vary according to the stretch fabric;
best to overestimate. Remember that
garment needs to be tight to stay
re.

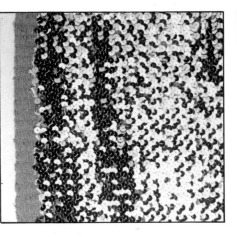

1 Pin the ends together and try on the boob tube for fit. Trim away any excess, allowing ¾in (2cm)-wide seam allowances. Trim away the sequins from the right side along the length and width of the seam allowances.

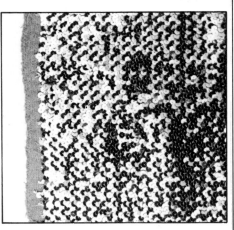

2 Finish the raw edges of the seam allowances with overcasting or zig-zag stitch.

ith right sides together, pin, baste and
h the seam using a zipper foot.
ure the stitching very firmly at each
. Use a stretch stitch on stretch fabric.

4 Press the seam open very gently with the tip of the iron, following the seamline.

5 Catch-stitch the seam allowances to the main fabric with tiny stitches that do not show on the right side.

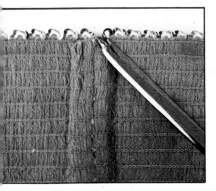

im away a small piece of the seam
wance on each side of the seam on
and bottom edges, so that the seam
wances do not show on the right
e of the garment.

7 Firmly catch-stitch the trimmed ends at the top and bottom of the seam firmly to the main fabric.

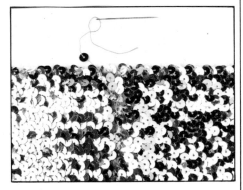

8 The top can be worn with the seam on one side or at the center back. If necessary, attach extra sequins to the seamline on the right side to hide the seam.

oat and eight-gore irt (1)

spangled outfit will see you ugh many a festive evening. have used chiffon but you ld try crepe with satin trim.

pting the pattern

urements

oat and skirt are adapted from the jacket and skirt patterns from the n by Stitch Pattern Pack, available es 10 to 20 (sizes 8-18 in ready- clothes).

rials

sheets of tracing paper 36×40in (90×40in), flexible curve ght triangle; yardstick

t

r the back bodice pattern, trace the t back pattern to just below the tline. Measure down the center edge from neck seamline, 16in m) for a size 10, adding an extra 5mm) to this measurement for each r size.
rk the back yoke line, measuring n center back edge from neck cutting er back edge from neck cutting line, 12.5cm) for a size 10, adding extra $\frac{1}{4}$in (5mm) to this measurement ach larger size. Draw the yoke line ss the pattern from this point at the er back to the armhole edge.
aw a line through the center of the lder dart down to the yoke line.
raw the dart stitching lines from the ning lines at the shoulder seam to yoke line as shown.

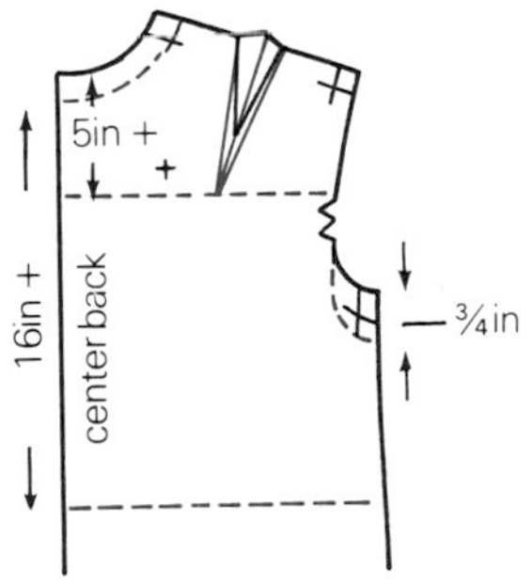

5in
16in
center back
¾in

wer the armhole by measuring down eamline $\frac{3}{4}$in (2cm) from the armhole ng line. Using a flexible curve, raw this part of the armhole curve, ring into the original cutting line at otches. Cut away the back neck n allowances, as this edge is to be nd.

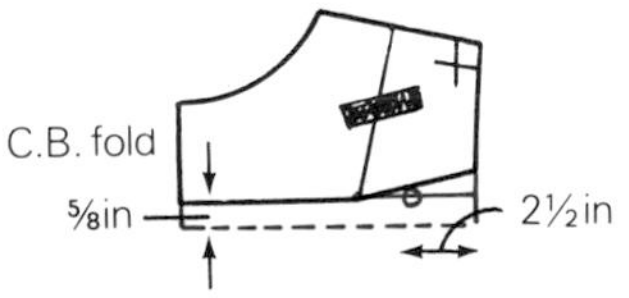

C.B. fold
⅝in
2½in

5 For the back yoke pattern, cut along the yoke line to separate the pattern. Close the shoulder dart and tape in place. Straighten the lower edge of the yoke and add $\frac{5}{8}$in (1.5cm) seam allowance to this edge. On the bottom seamline, mark the gathering position $2\frac{1}{2}$in (6.5cm) in from the armhole cutting line.
6 For the back bodice pattern add 1in (2.5cm) to the waistline edge of the pattern for the blousing allowance and a further $\frac{5}{8}$in (1.5cm) for seam allowance. Cut along the waist cutting line. For the gathering allowance, add $3\frac{1}{4}$in (8cm) to center back edge and $\frac{5}{8}$in (1.5cm) seam allowance to the top edge. Mark the gathering position on the top seamline $2\frac{1}{2}$in (6.5cm) in from armhole cutting line.

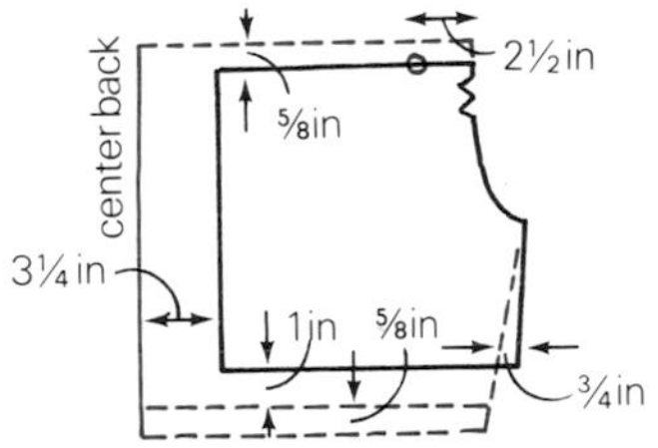

center back
2½in
⅝in
3¼in
1in
⅝in
¾in

7 At the lower edge take $\frac{3}{4}$in (2cm) off at side seam. Draw the new side cutting line from the lower edge, tapering into the original cutting line at the armhole.
8 For the front bodice pattern, trace the jacket front pattern piece to just below the waistline. To make the waistline, close the bust dart and lay the pattern over the back bodice with the side seams in line, marking the length of the center front. Mark the waistline and the seam allowance across the pattern. Lower the armhole by $\frac{3}{4}$in (2cm) as directed for the back.
9 At the shoulder seam and waist seam mark the neck and front seam allowances. Draw the new "V" neckline from the shoulder to the front edges as shown. A seam allowance is not required on this edge, as it is bound. Cut along the new neckline.

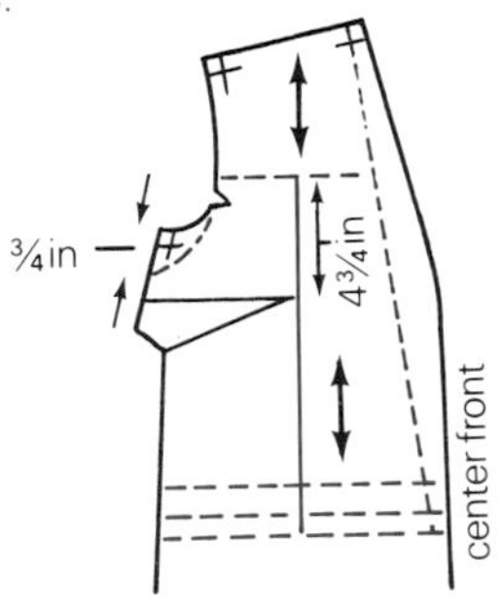

¾in
4¾in
center front

10 From the dart point draw upward a vertical line $4\frac{3}{4}$in (12cm) long; extend the line to the lower edge of the pattern. At the top of this line, draw the yoke line at a right angle as shown. Mark the grain line on the yoke parallel to the original grain line.

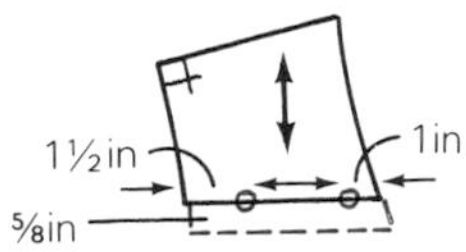

1½in
1in
⅝in

11 For the front yoke pattern, cut along the yoke line to separate the pattern. Add $\frac{5}{8}$in (1.5cm) seam allowance to the bottom edge of the yoke. Mark the gathering positions on the bottom seamline $1\frac{1}{2}$in (4cm) in from the armhole and 1in (2.5cm) in from the front edge.
12 For the front bodice pattern, lay the front bodice over paper, ready to tape in place. Slash through the pattern along the vertical line. Close the bust dart and tape in place. Open the pattern by $1\frac{1}{2}$in (4cm) at top edge, $\frac{5}{8}$in (1.5cm) at dart point and $2\frac{3}{4}$in (7cm) at the lower edge. Insert paper and tape in place.

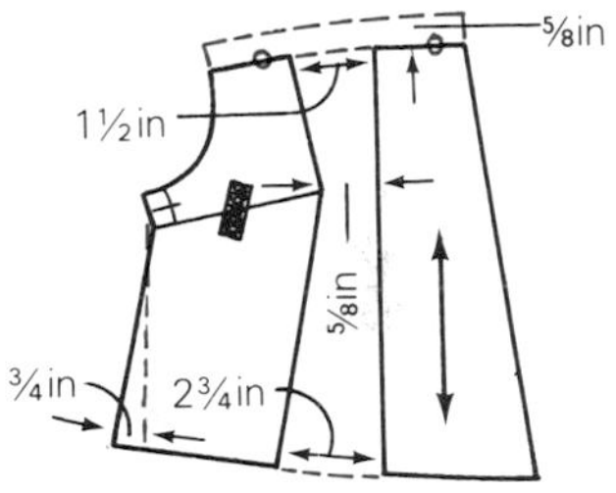

⅝in
1½in
⅝in
¾in
2¾in

13 Add $\frac{5}{8}$in (1.5cm) seam allowance to the top edge. For the gathering positions mark the seamline as directed for the yoke. Take $\frac{3}{4}$in (2cm) from the side seam edge at the lower edge, tapering the cutting line into the original cutting line at the armhole.
14 For the skirt back pattern, trace the basic skirt pattern. Take off 2in (5cm) at the lower edge; a $\frac{5}{8}$in (1.5cm) hem allowance has been included. Add $\frac{5}{8}$in (1.5cm) to side seam edge at the waistline, tapering the new cutting line into the original cutting line at hip level.

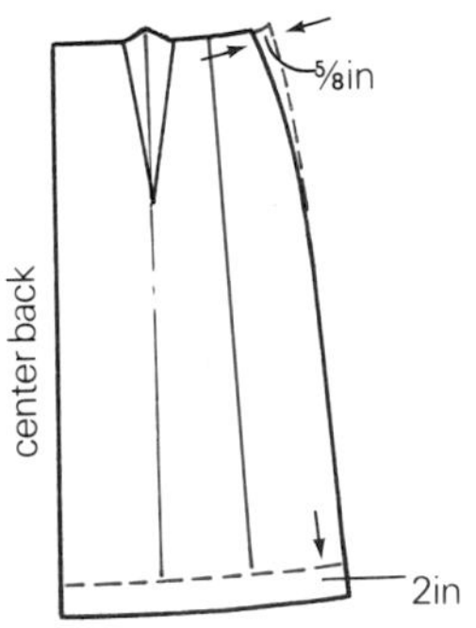

⅝in
center back
2in

15 Draw a vertical line through the center of the dart to the lower edge of the pattern. Draw another vertical line from top to bottom edges of the pattern between this line and side cutting line.

John Hutchinson

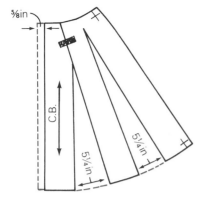

16 From the lower edge, slash along the first vertical line to the dart point. Close the dart and tape in place to open the pattern. Slash along the second vertical line up to the waist seam, and spread the pattern by $5\frac{1}{4}$in (13cm) between the slashes at the lower edge. Insert paper behind the slashes and tape in place. Add $\frac{5}{8}$in (1.5cm) seam allowance to the center back edge. Mark the grain line parallel to the center back.

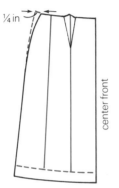

17 For the skirt front pattern, trace the basic skirt front, taking off 2in (5cm) at hem as for the back. Add $\frac{1}{4}$in (5mm) to side seam edge at the waistline, tapering into the original cutting line at hip level.

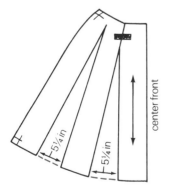

18 Draw the two vertical lines, slash and open the pattern following the directions for the skirt back. A seam allowance is not required at the center front edge, as this is to be bound. Mark the grain line parallel to the center front edge.
19 For the sleeve pattern, trace the jacket sleeve pattern, leaving extra paper at the lower edge. Lengthen the pattern by 12in

...cm) for a size 10, adding an extra ...mm) to this measurement for each ...size.

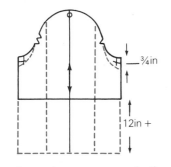

...wer the underarm curve on both ...dges of the sleeve by measuring ...the underarm seams ¾in (2cm) ...the cutting line and mark. Using a ...le curve, re-draw this part of the ..., tapering the line into the original ...ng the line at the notches. Extend ...rain line to the top and lower edges ...raw two parallel vertical lines ...ing each half of the sleeve as shown.

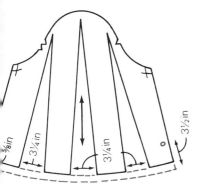

...ay the sleeve pattern over paper. ...n along the three vertical lines from ...ower edge up to the seamline at the ...ve cap. Spread the pattern by 3¼in ...n) between each slash at the lower ...e. Tape in place. Add ⅝in (1.5cm) ...n allowance to lower edge. Mark the ...n line down the center of the sleeve. ...k the length of the opening at the ...erarm seams 3½in (8.5cm) up from ...ower cutting line.

...or the cuff pattern, draw a rectangle ...10in (9.5×25cm) for a size 10, ...ng an extra ⅜in (1cm) to the length ...ach larger size.

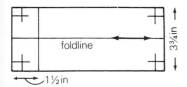

...Mark the ⅝in (1.5cm) seam allowance ...ll edges. Mark the foldline/grain line ...ng the center of the rectangle. At one ...mark the extension for the cuff ...ening, 1½in (4cm) in from the original ...ing line.

Sash

1 For the sash pattern, draw a rectangle 4¾in × 1½yd (12×130cm). Mark the rectangle into three sections, measuring 14½in (37cm) from one end (which will be the narrow end) and then a further 4½in (11cm). The remaining section of the rectangle will be the part which ties around the waist.

Note The sash can be worn on the skirt or coat; it is tied around the waist twice.

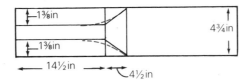

2 At the narrow end, mark the shaping with two horizontal lines 1⅜in (3.5cm) from top and bottom lines as far as the first vertical line. Connect each line to the top and bottom point of the second vertical line, curving the lines as shown.

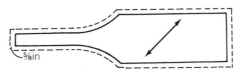

3 Add on ⅝in (1.5cm) seam allowance all around the pattern piece. Use a right triangle to mark the grain line on the bias as shown.

Eight-gore skirt

The pattern is based on T-shaped guide-lines as shown.

1 The length of the vertical line is the length of the skirt. This will be 28½in (72cm) for a size 10; add an extra ¼in (5mm) to this measurement for each larger size. Draw a horizontal line at hip level 8in (20.5cm) from the top edge. Draw a horizontal line at waist level.

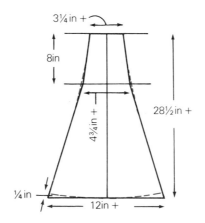

2 The first measurement given for each size is the waist measurement, the second

that at the hip and the last at the hem. Halve the measurements and mark them on each side of the vertical line: size 10: 3¼/4¾/12in (8/12/30cm). Add an extra ¼in (5mm) to each measurement for each size up through size 14. Size 16: 4/5½/12½in (10/14/32cm). Add ¼in (5mm) throughout for each larger size.

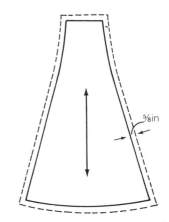

3 Connect these three points on each side of the vertical line to form the panel as shown, smoothing out the angles at the hip. At the lower edge, curve the hem up ¼in (5mm) at each side. Add ⅝in (1.5cm) seam allowance to all edges. Mark the grain line through the center of the panel. Mark zipper point 8in (20.5cm) from waist seam on two panels only.

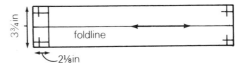

4 For the waistband pattern, draw a rectangle 3¾in (9.5cm) wide by the following lengths: 28in (71cm) for size 10; 29½in (75cm) for size 12; 31in (79cm) for size 14; 34¼in (87cm) for size 16; 36in (91cm) for size 18; 37½in (95cm) for size 20.
These measurements include a 1½in (4cm) extension for fastening and ⅝in (1.5cm) seam allowance on all edges. Mark the seam allowances and foldline. The grain line will follow the foldline in the center of the rectangle.
Directions for assembling the outfit are in the next course.

*Applying sequins
*Making and applying a
  sequined motif
*Pattern for coat and
  eight-gore skirt (2):
  directions for making

Applying sequins

Never attempt to sew sequins on a domestic sewing machine, for you will break either the needle or the sequins. Sequins can be applied in a row, either directly from the card or—in the case of loose sequins—threaded first by hand onto a single thread to form a length; they can also be applied individually. Choose the method to suit the motif or garment.

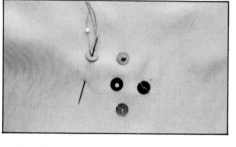

1 Sequins sewn on singly can be sewn across the sequin and into the hole or applied with a small bead in the center. Secure the thread on the wrong side of the fabric. Bring the needle through the center of the sequin and the back over the bead. The bead acts as an anchor for the thread. Fasten the thread securely in the fabric.

2 To apply sequins in a strand, sew the first sequin of the row firmly throu~~gh~~ the center hole to hold it. Taking a longish stitch beneath the fabric, brin~~g~~ the needle up between two sequins, t~~o~~ one side of the stranding thread. Take ~~the~~ needle across and into the fabric to ho~~ld~~ the stranding thread in place. Aim to sew the thread down between every second or third sequin. Sew the last sequin firmly to hold it in place.

Making and applying a sequined motif

There are various methods of making a sequined motif, but generally each method will employ one or both of the techniques shown above; the sequins are applied either singly to build up a block shape, or in a strand following an outline. The coat on page 61 has a number of motifs worked over the yoke, bodice and sleeve area, using strands of sequins for the outline of the flower and leaves, and individually-applied sequins for the centers. The shape of the motif used here is intended as a guide only, as the beauty of the design lies in its random shapes and sizes.

When sewing the motifs, work from th~~e~~ right side, stretching the piece of fabri~~c~~ in an embroidery frame. If applying a motif to a shoulder area, it is advisable ~~to~~ seam the shoulder or yoke pieces first. Beads can be added for extra decorati~~on.~~

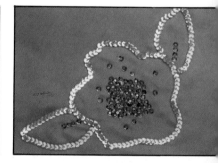

1 Pin or tape the section of fabric to be sequined to a flat surface such as a cork tile or clean white paper over layers of newspaper on a table. Draw the outline of the motif with a dressmaker's pencil or tailor's chalk. On sheer fabric, the outline can be traced from a drawing.

2 Starting with the outlines, apply the stranded sequins as shown above. Sew down the starting and finishing sequins very securely. Complete all the outlines on the garment first, and check the balance of the design before adding more sequins.

3 When the outlines are complete, continue applying sequins individually ~~to~~ the centers as shown above, building up a block. All pencil marks should be covered by the sequins. If the center of the motif is to be heavily covered and th~~e~~ material is very flimsy, use a small piec~~e of~~ the lightest weight interfacing to back t~~he~~ fabric before applying the sequins.

Coat and eight-gore skirt (2)

Here we continue the directions for the coat and skirt featured on page 52. We have used harmonizing fabrics of one color throughout, but you could choose contrasting trim.

Directions for making

Suggested fabrics
Chiffon, georgette, crepe, crepe-de-chine. Lining and bindings: china silk, crepe de chine, polyester lining-type fabrics.

Materials
Skirt
45in (115cm)-wide fabric without nap:
Sizes 10,12: 2¼yd (2m)
Sizes 14, 16: 2⅝yd (2.3m)
Sizes 18, 20: 2⅝yd (2.4m)
36in (90cm)-wide lining fabric:
Sizes 10, 12: 2⅝yd (2.4m)
Sizes 14, 16: 2⅞yd (2.6m)
Sizes 18, 20: 3yd (2.7m)
36in (90cm)-wide interfacing:
for all sizes: ⅛yd (.1m)
8in (20cm) nylon zipper
2 hooks and eyes
Sequins (amount varies according to method of application)

Coat
45in (115cm)-wide fabric without nap:
Sizes 10, 12: 4⅛yd (3.7m)
Sizes 14, 16: 4¼yd (3.9m)
Sizes 18, 20: 4⅜yd (4m)
45in (115cm)-wide fabric for sash and binding:
for all sizes 2⅝yd (2.3m)
36in (90cm)-wide interfacing:
for all sizes: ⅛yd (.1m)
1 hook and eye
4 snaps
Sequins

Key to adjusted pattern pieces

A	Back yoke	Cut 2 on fold
B	Back bodice	Cut 1 on fold
C	Front yoke	Cut 4
D	Front bodice	Cut 2
E	Coat skirt back	Cut 2
F	Coat skirt front	Cut 2
G	Sleeve	Cut 2
H	Cuff	Cut 2
I	Sash	Cut 4
J	Skirt	Cut 8
K	Waistband	Cut 1

Interfacing: Use pieces **H** Cut 2 to half width only, **K** Cut 1 to half width only.

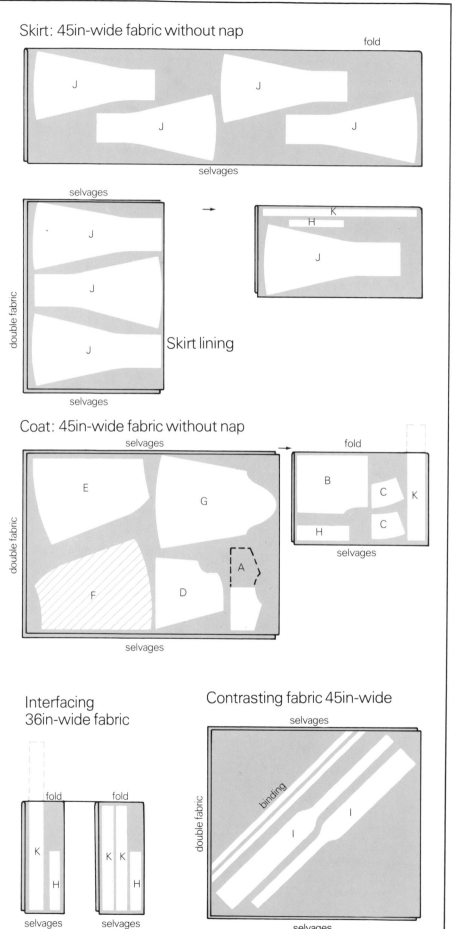

Skirt: 45in-wide fabric without nap

J J J J

fold

selvages

Skirt lining

selvages

J J J

double fabric

selvages

K
H
J

Coat: 45in-wide fabric without nap

selvages

E G

F D A

double fabric

selvages

fold

B C K
H C

selvages

Interfacing
36in-wide fabric

fold fold

K K K
H H

selvages selvages

Contrasting fabric 45in-wide

selvages

binding

I I

I

double fabric

selvages

Skirt

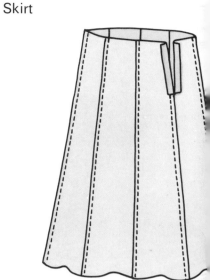

1 Stitch panels together using French seam method (see Volume 13, page 83 leaving left seam open $8\frac{1}{2}$in (22cm) for zipper.
2 Press all seams to one side and clip into the seam allowance at the bottom the zipper opening.

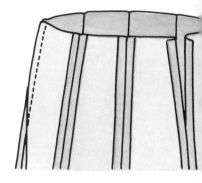

3 Make the lining in the same way, but use plain open seams, leaving $8\frac{1}{2}$in (22cm) open at the left side edge. Finis the seam allowances and press the seams open.

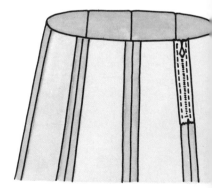

4 Slip the lining over the skirt, right side of lining to wrong side of skirt and seam and openings matching; baste the lining to the skirt at the waist edge. Treating the lining and skirt as one, press the opening allowances flat to the inside and insert zipper by hand, preferably using prick stitch (see Volume 2, page 4

Ian Stephen

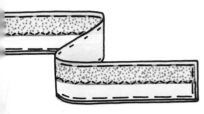

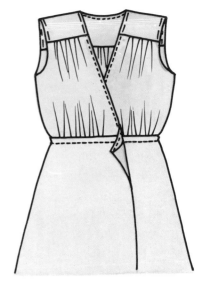

ste the lining to the wrong side of
waistband. The lining prevents the
facing or belt stiffening from showing
ugh. Baste the interfacing to the
stband over the lining and catch-stitch
e foldline.

th right sides together, baste and
h the waistband to the skirt, with
extension at the back edge of the
ning. Grade the seam allowances;
interfacing close to stitching, and
s toward waistband.

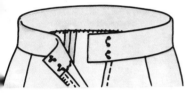

old the waistband right sides together
ng the foldline and stitch across the
s. Grade the seam allowances and
across corners.
rn the waistband right side out and
te close to the folded edge. On the
de, turn under the seam allowance
he waistband and slip stitch it to the
ching line. Sew two hooks and eyes
he waistband.

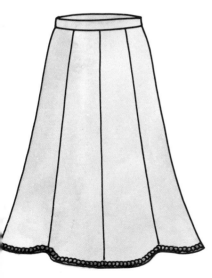

t the lower edge of the skirt turn under
(1cm) and a further ⅜in (1cm) and

baste. Hem by hand. Remove basting
and press. Apply sequins to the lower
edge of the skirt by the single strand or
individually-sewn method (see page
56). Let the skirt hang for a few days
before completing the lining hem in the
same way (omitting sequins). The
lining should be ⅜in (1cm) shorter than
the skirt.

Coat

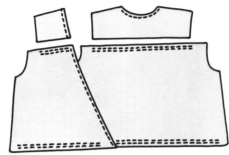

1 Staystitch the neck edge of the front
and back yokes and bodices. Run two
rows of gathering stitches between
marks at the top edge of bodices and
across the lower edge of bodices.

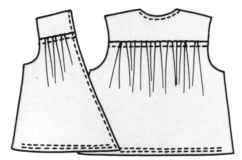

2 With right sides together, pin the front
and back yokes to the corresponding
bodices, pulling up the gathering threads
to fit. Baste, spreading the gathers evenly.
Stitch seams and trim them to ⅜in (1cm).
Overcast seams to finish. Press seams
toward yokes.

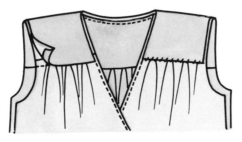

3 With right sides together, baste and
stitch shoulder seams of yokes and yoke
facings. Press seams open. With wrong
sides together and shoulder seams and
neck and armhole edges matching, baste
the yoke facings to the inside of yokes at
neck and armhole edges. Turn under the
seam allowances at the bottom edges of
yoke facings and slip stitch them to the
yoke stitching lines.

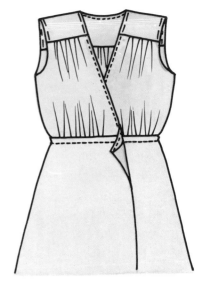

4 Using French seams (see Volume 13,
page 83) stitch the side seams of bodice
and coat pieces. Press all seams toward
the back.
5 With right sides together and side
seams, center fronts and center backs
matching, pin bodice to coat skirt at the
waistline, pulling up the gathering
threads until the bodice fits. Baste,
spreading gathers evenly around waist.
Stitch seam and trim to ⅜in (1cm).

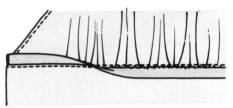

6 Cut a bias strip of self fabric, 1½in
(4cm) wide, to bind the waist seam
allowance. Bind the seam allowance
(see Volume 1, page 56). Press it upward.
Turn up the hem as for the skirt, omitting
sequins.

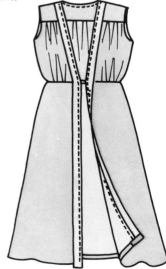

7 To bind the entire front and neck edges
of the coat, cut bias strips of contrasting

fabric 1½in (4cm) wide and join strips to make a piece long enough to bind these these edges.

8 Begin at the lower edge, leaving a seam allowance to turn under. With right sides together, baste binding to the center front and neck edges, taking a ⅜in (1cm) seam allowance. Stitch binding in place and press away from the coat. At the lower edge turn the binding up to the inside.

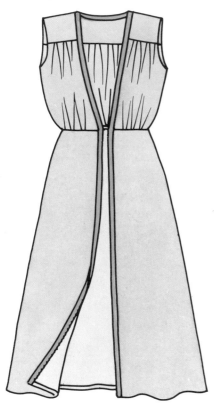

9 Turn binding to the inside over raw edges, turn under ⅜in (1cm) seam allowance of the binding and slip stitch it to the stitching line. Press carefully. Sew a hook and eye to the inside edge of binding at the waist.

10 Run two rows of gathering threads around sleeve cap between notches. Stitch underarm seam of sleeve with a French seam, leaving the seam open at the lower edge.

These motifs can be drawn freehand on the right side of the fabric with a dressmaker's pencil. Place the fabric on a hard, flat surface. The pattern is intended as a guide only; the motifs are intended to be finished in a random way so that each flower differs slightly from the others.

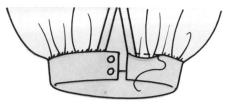

13 With right sides together, fold cuff and stitch across ends. Trim seam allowances. Cut across corners. Turn cuff right side out and baste around outer edges. Turn under cuff seam allowance and slip stitch to the stitching line. Press.
Sew two snaps to cuff. Repeat for second sleeve.

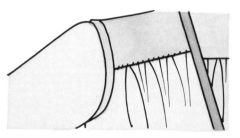

14 With right sides together and seams and shoulder points matching, baste and stitch sleeve into armhole. Clip curves and trim seam to $\frac{3}{8}$in (1cm). Finish seams with self fabric bias binding as directed for waist seam.

Sash

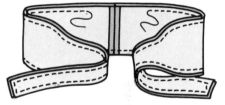

1 With right sides together, baste and stitch sash center seams. Lay the sash pieces flat and handle as little as possible until stitched, to prevent them from stretching out of shape. With right sides together, stitch sashes together, leaving an opening in one long edge.

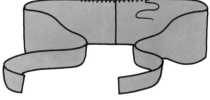

2 Turn sash right side out and baste around stitched edges. Press. Turn in the seam allowance at the opening and slip stitch the edges together. Press.
3 Complete the coat with sequined motifs (following the trace patterns) applied at random over the bodice, yokes and sleeves, using one of the methods shown on page 56.

above the opening.
s seam allowance toward front edge
e sleeve.
taystitch around the opening and
the seam allowance of the opening
n (1cm). Cut a bias strip of self
c 1½in (4cm) wide, to bind the
ning. Bind the opening using the
d slit method (see Volume 5, page
Press front binding to the inside edge
eeve and the back binding flat. Run
rows of gathering stitches around the
er edge of the sleeve, pulling up the
ering threads until sleeve fits cuff.

12 Baste the lining to the wrong side of the cuff. Baste the interfacing to the cuff over the lining. Catch stitch it to the foldline. With right sides together, pin sleeve to interfacing edge of cuff, pulling up gathers to fit. The extension of cuff is at back edge of sleeve. Baste, spreading gathers evenly. Stitch seam. Trim seam and press toward cuff.

Terry Evans

Shoestring

Border lines

Bright, patterned ribbons add special interest to a simple blouse. Use one wide ribbon or several narrow ones, as shown here.

Materials
    Blouse
    Patterned and/or solid color ribbons (for amounts see step 1)
    Matching thread

1 Decide which parts of the blouse would look good trimmed with ribbon. Measure each seam or edge and add ¾in (2cm) to each measurement for turning under at the ends. Add the measurements to get the total required. Round up the figure slightly to allow for shrinkage, if necessary.

3 If the garment is washable, first immerse the ribbon in hand-hot water a few minutes to shrink it. Allow it to then iron it. Also wash and iron the blouse, if it is new.

3 If there are any buttons or other fastenings on the blouse that might ge the way of the stitching, remove them temporarily.

4 Cut the ribbon to fit the seams or edges, allowing extra as specified in s 1.

5 Pin and baste each length of ribbon place, turning under 3/8in (1cm) at ea end and basting down the center of th ribbon.

6 Topstitch close to the edges, makir sure that the raw ends are caught und the stitching.

7 When all the ribbons have been stitched on, re-sew the buttons to the blouse.

* Tie fastenings
* Applying an overlaid gusset
* Pattern for a maternity
  smock:
  adapting the pattern;
  directions for making

fastenings

astenings are attractive and easy to
. The opening can be edge to edge
verlapped simply by adjusting the
ment of the ties. On the smock on
64, we have made the ties to a

finished width of $\frac{5}{8}$in (1.5cm) but you
could make them wider if you wish.
For neck ties, cut two strips 14×2in
(35×5cm) finished size: 13×$\frac{5}{8}$in [33×
1.5cm]); for the wrist ties, cut four

strips 8×2in (20×5cm) (finished size:
7×$\frac{5}{8}$in [18×1.5cm]).
Here the ties match the contrasting
binding, but they could be made in self
fabric to match the main garment.

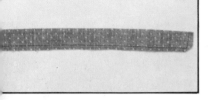

right sides together, fold the strip
f lengthwise. Stitch along the
and one short end, taking a $\frac{3}{8}$in
) seam. Trim seam to $\frac{1}{4}$in (5mm)
ip corner. Press.

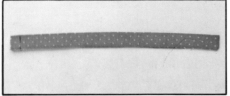

2 Turn right side out and turn in the
raw ends. Baste across the end to hold
the raw ends in place and press gently.

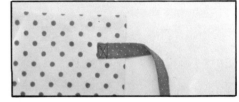

3 Center the strip over the opening with
the basted end approximately 1$\frac{1}{4}$in (3cm)
in from the edge of the opening. Baste
to hold and topstitch a $\frac{5}{8}$in (1.5cm)
square. Stitch diagonals for strength.
Secure threads on wrong side. Remove
basting and press.

lying an overlaid gusset

ets are squares or triangles of cloth
to seams of garments at points of
to give extra room. The gusset can
ade to any size, but the seam into
it is to be set must be left unstitched

for the appropriate length. Be very careful
when stitching the overlaid gusset to
ensure that it is caught firmly on the seam
allowances below. On the smock on page
64, we have used a diamond-shaped

gusset in a contrasting fabric. If you were
using this technique to add fullness to
a ready-made garment, you could use a
matching fabric, which would be practic-
ally invisible.

out the gusset shape to the given
vith the grain following the points.
n $\frac{5}{8}$in (1.5cm) seam allowances to
rong side all around, and baste to
If the fabric is bulky, the corners can
tered, but do not clip right into the
as this will cause weakness
gusset.

2 Make the sleeve and bodice and set
the sleeve into the armhole, following
the directions on page 70. Leave the
underarm seam of sleeve and bodice
at armhole edges open for approximately
2in (5cm), to take the gusset. Pin the
gusset in place, overlaying it on the right
side of the underarm seams. Match each
point to the ends of the seam stitching
and the edges of the gusset to the
seamlines.

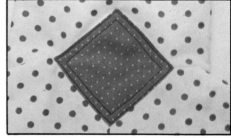

3 Baste all around through gusset and
garment fabric. Machine-stitch all around
close to edges of gusset and again
$\frac{1}{4}$in (5mm) away from first line of
stitching. Remove basting and press
gently.

Simon Butcher

Belinda

Maternity smock

This versatile smock in two versions would be a useful addition to your wardrobe during those waiting months. The easy shape is flattering to any fuller figure.

Adapting the pattern

Measurements
The pattern for the smock is adapted from the basic shirt from the Stitch by Stitch Pattern Pack, available in sizes 10 to 20, which correspond to sizes 8 to 18 in ready-made clothes. To make the smock for maternity wear, use one size larger than usual. There will be no size 20.

Materials
*4 sheets of tracing paper 35 × 40in
(90 × 100cm)
Flexible curve
Yardstick; right triangle*

1 Pin the front and back yokes to the shirt front and back, overlapping the $\frac{5}{8}$in (1.5cm) seam allowance so that the seamlines are aligned. Trace the complete pattern pieces.

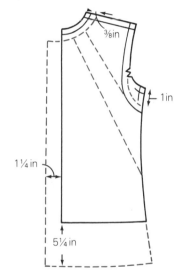

2 For the back pattern, lower the armhole curve by 1in (2.5cm) tapering into the original line at the notches. Mark the seam allowance around the armhole, shoulder and neck edges.
3 To make the neckline larger, mark the new neckline $\frac{3}{8}$in (1cm) from the original seamline around the complete neck edge. A seam allowance is not needed at the neck, which is to be bound, so trim away excess pattern.
4 Divide the neck seamline into three equal parts and draw two slash lines as shown; one to the deepest part of the armhole curve, and one to the middle of the side seam. Add 1$\frac{1}{4}$in (3cm) to the center back edge and lengthen the pattern by 5$\frac{1}{4}$in (13cm) at lower edge, adjusting the length if necessary.

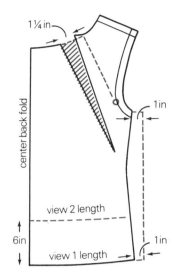

5 Slash down the line from neck edge to the side seam. Spread the pattern by 1$\frac{1}{4}$in (3cm) at neck edge. Insert paper behind slash and tape it in place. Re-draw this part of the neck edge as shown. For extra fullness, add 1in (2.5cm) to the side seam edge at top and bottom. Connect points with a straight line.
6 Mark shorter length (View 2) 6in (15cm) up from the cutting line at the lower edge. Mark the point at the armhole seamline where the second line drawn from the neck meets the armhole seam. This line will become the raglan seamline.

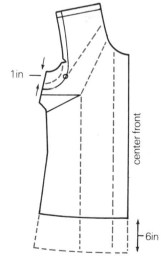

7 For the front pattern, lower the armhole, make neck larger, lengthen pattern and mark View 2 length, following measurements and directions given for the back. Mark the seamline around armhole and shoulder. Trim away excess pattern at neck edge.

John Hutchinson

8 Divide the front neck seamline into four equal parts. The first line is drawn to the deepest part of the armhole curve. This will become the seamline for the raglan. Mark a circle where the line crosses the armhole seamline. The second line goes to the dart point and continues down to the lower edge, parallel to the center front. The third line is from the neck seamline to the lower edge, approximately 1½in (4cm) in from the center front.

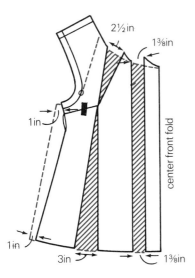

9 Slash along the second line from the neck to the dart point and then from the lower edge to the dart point, without separating the pattern completely at this point. Close the side bust dart and tape in place. This will open pattern by 2½in (6.5cm) at neck edge and 3in (7.5cm) at lower edge. Insert and tape paper behind the slashes. Slash along the third line from top and bottom edge of the pattern and only by 1⅜in (3.5cm). Insert and tape paper behind slash. Add 1in (2.5cm) to side seam edge at top and bottom. Connect these points with a straight line.

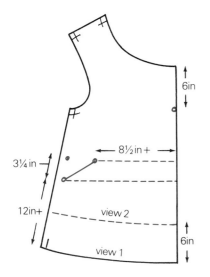

10 For the pocket position, measure up side seamline 12in (30cm) for sizes

10 to **14**; 12½in (32cm) for larger sizes. Mark a further 3¼in (8cm) for depth of pocket. Draw two horizontal lines across pattern to connect center front to these points, but make top line slightly shorter— 8½in (22cm) for sizes 10 to 12; 9¼in (23.5cm); 14 to 16; 10in (25cm); 18. The lower line is drawn to the side seamline. Connect these two marks for the pocket line.

11 Mark the length of the center front opening 6in (15cm) below the neck edge. Re-draw the neck as shown in step 9. This does not need a seam allowance, as it is to be bound. There is no hem allowance included in the length, as the hem edge, also, is to be bound on both versions.

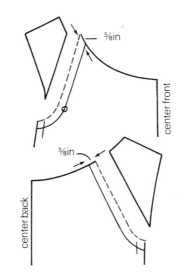

12 Cut along the upper slash lines (nearest the shoulder) to separate the shoulder sections from the front and back pieces. Trim away the armhole and shoulder seam allowance. Add a ⅝in (1.5cm) seam allowance to raglan edge on the front and back smock pieces.

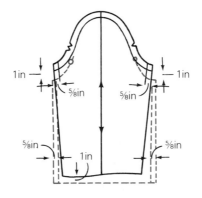

13 For the sleeve pattern, trace the shirt sleeve pattern, extending the grain line to the top and bottom of the pattern. Cut away the seam allowance around the sleeve cap. To make the sleeve cap larger, measure 1in (2.5cm) down the underarm seams from the *seamline* of the sleeve cap and extend seamline out by ⅝in (1.5cm). Mark these points. Using a

flexible curve, re-draw this part of the fr and back sleeve cap curve, tapering the seamlines into the original seamline at the notches.

14 Re-draw the underarm seamlines do to the lower edge of the pattern and ad 1in (2.5cm) to lower edge. Add ⅝in (1.5cm) seam allowance to the underarm seams.

15 On front and back patterns measure the distance from underarm seamline to the circles on raglan seamlines. Mark these measurements on the front and back armhole edges of sleeve, taking th measurement from the new underarm seamlines.

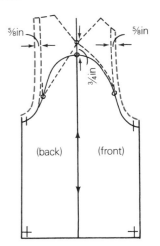

16 Extend the grain line beyond the top edge of the pattern. Position the front and back shoulder sections on each sid of the sleeve cap as shown, matching t points marked on the seamlines, with their shoulder points touching, ¾in (2c above the sleeve cap. The back shoulde section will overlap the sleeve cap slightly as shown. Tape the pieces in place. Add ⅝in (1.5cm) seam allowanc to raglan armhole edges.

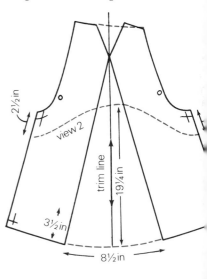

17 Some of the fullness at the neck edg of the sleeve is transferred to the lower edge; slash pattern along the grain line

e shoulder point and from the neck
 to the shoulder point, without
ng through pattern completely. Close
attern at the neck edge so that the
r edge opens by 8½in (22cm). Insert
r behind the slash and tape in place.
ghten the neck edge as shown.
Mark the strap positioning line down
enter of the sleeve. This will also
e grain line. Mark the sleeve opening
tion, 3½in (9cm) long, in the center
e back lower edge of the sleeve.
k View 2 lengths 19¼in (49cm) up
 the lower edge on the grain line,
2½in (6.5cm) down each side seam
 the armhole cutting line. Using a
ble curve, join these points in a
ed line as shown. View 2 sleeve does
have a hem allowance, as the sleeve
is to be finished with a contrasting
ing.

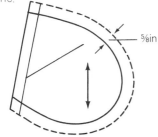

or the pocket bag pattern, using a
ble curve, draw the outline of the
ket shape on the smock front at the
tions marked in step 10. The deepest
of the pocket is 6in (15cm) from the
ket line.

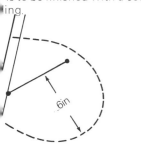

race the pocket shape onto paper
add ⅝in (1.5cm) seam allowance
e curved edge. Mark the grain line
llel to the center front.

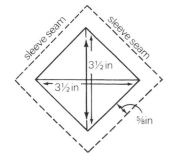

To make gusset, draw a diamond 3½in
m) across from point to point. Add
(1.5cm) seam allowances to edges.

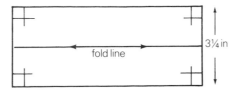

22 For cuff pattern, draw a rectangle
3¼ × 8½in (8 × 22cm) for a size 10 adding
an extra ⅜in (1cm) to length for each
larger size. These measurements include
⅝in (1.5cm) seam allowances on all
edges. Mark the foldline and the grain
line along the center of the rectangle.
23 For the front opening binding, draw
a rectangle 2in (5cm) wide by twice the
length of the opening. This piece will be
cut once on the bias.
24 For the sleeve opening binding, draw
a rectangle 2in (5cm) wide by twice the
length of the opening. This piece will be
cut twice on the bias.
25 For the pattern for trimming at the
armhole seam, measure the full length of
the front raglan seamline. Draw a
rectangle to this length by 2in (5cm)
wide. Measure the full length of the back
raglan seam and draw a rectangle to this
length by 2in (5cm) wide. Each piece will
be cut twice on the bias.

26 For the sleeve trimming pattern,
measure the length of the positioning
line, and cut a rectangle to this length by
2in (5cm) wide. This piece will be cut
twice on the straight grain.
27 For pocket bindings, measure length
of the pocket opening and draw a
rectangle to this length plus 1¼in (3cm)
by 4in (10cm) wide. This piece will be cut
twice on the straight grain.
28 For the neck binding, measure around
the neck edge after the garment body
sections have been joined and reduced
by gathering. Cut a rectangle to this
length plus 2in (5cm) by 3¼in (8cm)
wide. Cut this piece once on the bias.
29 For the sleeve binding of View 2,
measure the hem of the sleeve after the
underarm seams have been joined and
cut a piece to this length plus 1¼in
(3cm) by 3¼in (8cm) wide. This piece
will be cut twice on the bias.
30 For the hem binding, measure front
and back hemlines. Cut a rectangle to
this length by 3¼in (8cm) wide. Pieces
should be cut on the straight grain.
31 For the ties, cut strips 2in (5cm)
wide by length required for each strip
on the straight grain. The ties will be
⅝in (1.5cm) wide when finished but
may be adjusted for width.

Belinda

Directions for making

Materials

Long-sleeved version (view 1)
36 or 45in (90 or 115cm)-wide fabric without nap:
Sizes 10, 12: $3\frac{7}{8}$yd (3.5m)
Sizes 14, 16: 4yd (3.6m)
Sizes 18, 20: $4\frac{1}{8}$yd (3.7m)
Contrasting bindings and trim:
45in (115cm)-wide fabric without nap: $1\frac{3}{4}$yd (1.5m)
36in (90cm)-wide interfacing, for all sizes: $\frac{1}{4}$yd (.2m)
Short-sleeved version (view 2)
36 or 45in (90 or 115cm)-wide fabric with or without nap:
Sizes 10, 12: $2\frac{5}{8}$yd (2.5m)
Size 14: $2\frac{3}{4}$yd (2.5m)
Sizes 16, 18: $2\frac{7}{8}$yd (2.6m)
Size 20: 3yd (2.7m)
Contrasting binding and ties:
45in (115cm)-wide fabric without nap: $1\frac{1}{2}$yd (1.2m)
Matching thread

Suggested fabrics
Cotton poplin, lawn, light to medium-weight blends, velveteen. For evenings: satin or crepe.

Key to adjusted pattern pieces

Views 1 and 2

A	Smock back	Cut 1 on fold
B	Front	Cut 1 on fold
C	Sleeve	Cut 2
D	Pocket bag	Cut 2
E	Gusset	Cut 2
F	Front opening binding	Cut 1
G	Pocket binding	Cut 2
H	Neck binding	Cut 1
I	Neck ties	Cut 2
J	Hem binding	Cut 2
L	Armhole trim	Cut 4

View 1 only

K	Sleeve trim	Cut 2
M	Sleeve opening binding	Cut 2
N	Cuff	Cut 2
O	Wrist ties	Cut 4

Interfacing: use piece N cut 2 to half width only.

View 2 only

P	Sleeve hem binding	Cut 2

Note If necessary, join binding pieces to make up the length required for sleeve and hem bindings.

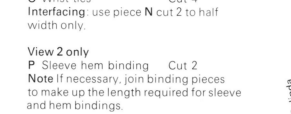

Belinda

View 1: Cutting layout for 36in or 45in-wide fabric without nap.

View 1: 45i

View 2: 36in or 45in-wide fabric with or without nap.

View 2: 45i

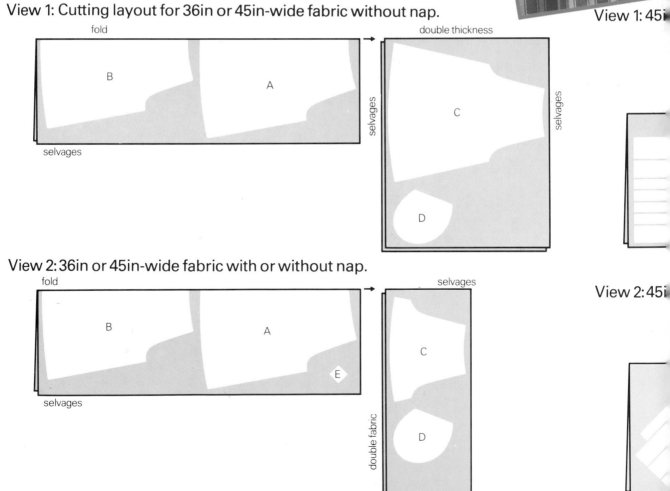

Brian Mayor

Long-sleeved version

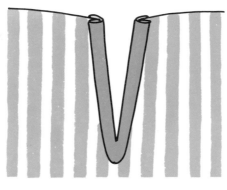

1 Staystitch around the center front opening. Complete the center front slit opening with binding as shown in Volume 8, page 54.

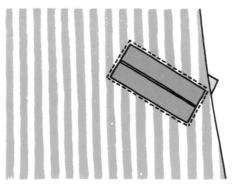

2 To bind the pockets, cut two strips of contrasting fabric on the straight grain 4in (10cm) wide and $1\frac{1}{4}$in (3cm) longer than the pocket opening. Apply the binding to the pocket openings as for bound buttonholes (see Volume 10, page 75). Stitch $\frac{5}{8}$in (1.5cm) from pocket line all around when completing. The finished bindings will be $\frac{5}{8}$in (1.5cm) deep. One end of the pocket opening will be stitched into the side seam when assembling garment (both versions).

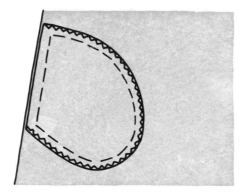

3 Overcast or zig-zag all around the curved edge of the pocket bag to finish. With right side of pocket bag to wrong side of garment, position the bag over the opening, matching straight edges at side. Baste $\frac{5}{8}$in (1.5cm) from the edges, including the side edges, to hold bag in place.

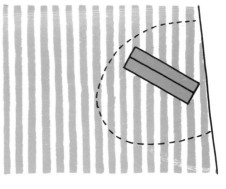

4 Make sure the opening is correctly placed over the bag shape. Machine-stitch over basting lines, keeping curves smooth. Remove basting and press.

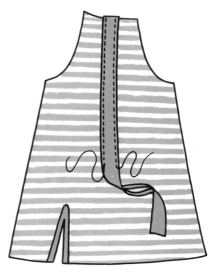

5 Staystitch around sleeve opening and apply binding as directed for neck opening.
6 Turn under $\frac{3}{8}$in (1cm) seam allowances along outer edges of sleeve trim pieces and press flat. Apply trim over positioning lines in center of sleeves and stitch in place as shown in Volume 12, page 75.

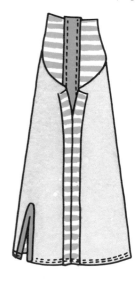

7 With right sides together, baste and stitch underarm seams to within 2in

ting fabric with or
nap.

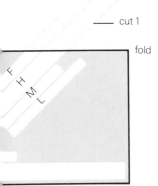

— cut 1

fold

F
H
M
L

selvages

with or without nap.

cut 1

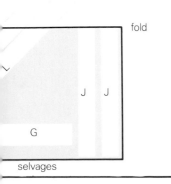

fold

J J

G

selvages

Terry Evans

(5cm) of the armhole seamline. Finish and press seam open. Run two rows of gathering stitches around lower edge of sleeves.

8 Baste interfacing to wrong side of cuffs and catch-stitch to fold lines. With right sides together, pin sleeve to cuff, pulling up gathers until sleeve fits. Baste, spreading the gathers evenly. Stitch seam. Trim interfacing close to stitching and trim seams. Press seam allowance toward cuff.

9 With right sides together, fold cuff along foldline and stitch across ends. Trim interfacing and seam allowances. Cut across the corners before turning right side out.

10 Turn cuff right side out and baste close to folded edge. Press. On the inside, turn under the seam allowances of cuff and slip stitch to the stitching line. Press. Repeat with the second cuff.

11 Make and apply the wrist ties as directed on page 63. The finished width of the ties will be $\frac{5}{8}$in (1.5cm) and their length, 7in (18cm). The ties are cut on the straight grain, as this gives extra strength to the pieces.

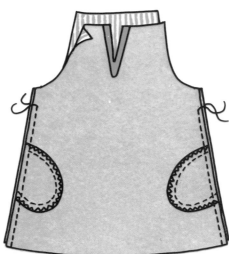

12 With right sides together, baste and stitch side seams to within 2in (5cm) of armhole seamline. Finish and press seams open.

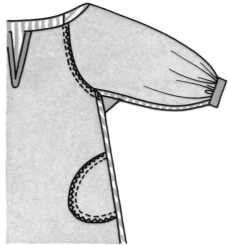

13 With right sides together, baste and stitch sleeves into armholes. Trim seams to $\frac{3}{8}$in (1cm) and clip curves. Finish seams together and press toward sleeve.

14 Cut four bias strips of contrasting fabric 2in (5cm) wide and the length of

each armhole seamline (front and ba[ck] for the armhole trim—four pieces in a[ll]. Turn under $\frac{3}{8}$in (1cm) seam allowanc[e] each long edge and press flat. With ri[ght] sides on top, center trim over raglan seams and stitch in place, stitching cl[ose] to the edges of the binding. Press. Make and apply the gussets to the underarm seams at the armholes as s[hown] on page 63, making sure the gussets f[it] openings.

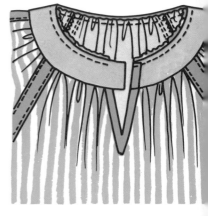

15 Run two rows of gathering aroun[d] entire neck edge. Pull up gathering until neck measures 18in (46cm) for sizes 10 and 12; $19\frac{1}{4}$in (49cm) for siz[es] 14 and 16; $20\frac{1}{2}$in (52cm) for size 18.

16 Cut a bias strip of contrasting fab[ric] 2in (5cm) longer than neck measure[ment] by $3\frac{1}{4}$in (8cm) wide. With right sides together, pin to neck edge, positioni[ng] binding edge of neck $\frac{1}{4}$in (5mm) outs[ide] neck edge. Baste and stitch in place, taking $\frac{3}{8}$in (1cm) seam. Grade seams clip curves almost to stitching line.

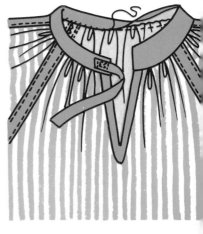

17 Press binding toward neck edge. Turn in the seam allowance at the fro[nt] edges of binding. Turn binding to ins[ide] over seam allowance and slip stitch t[o] stitching line. Press carefully; the finished width of binding is 1in (2.5c[m]) on both smocks.

18 Make and apply two ties as direct[ed] on page 63 and stitch to binding at ce[nter] front opening. Ties have a finished le[ngth] of 13in (33cm).

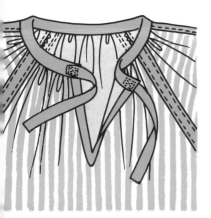

...ut two strips of contrasting fabric
... (8cm) wide by length of front and
...hem edges, plus seam allowances.
... to form a ring. If necessary cut more
...two pieces to make up length.

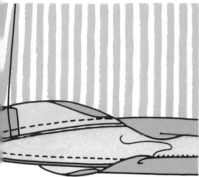

...ith right sides together and side
...s matching, baste binding to hem
... taking $\frac{5}{8}$in (1.5cm) seam. Press
...ng down and turn to inside over
...n allowance. On the inside, turn under
...ng and slip stitch to stitching line.
...s. Finished width of binding is 1in
...cm).

...ort-sleeved version

...e as for long-sleeved version,
...ting vertical sleeve trim, cuff and
...t ties. Bind sleeve hems as directed
...em of smock, using bias strips 3$\frac{1}{4}$in
...n) wide to make a finished width of
...2.5cm).

Belinda

Waist tie

A knitted necktie make:
novel belt, with the additio
a buckle and a few eyelets

Materials

Knitted necktie
Buckle to fit width of tie
Several metal eyelets
Dressmaker's marking pencil
Matching thread
Scrap of iron-on interfacing
(optional)

1 Wrap the tie around your waist to check the length. If it is too long, cut away the excess from the middle of the tie. The narrow end of the tie, which will hold the buckle, should measure half the waist measurement, plus a little more than 1in (2.5cm) from the seam (center back) to the end; the wider end should measure half the waist measurement plus the desired overlap.

2 Stitch the two cut ends together. Finish the seam allowances by overcasting them to the underside of the tie as shown, so that they will lie flat.

3 At the narrow end of the tie, mark the center, 1in (2.5cm) from the end, using the dressmaker's pencil. Fix an eyelet at this point, following the manufacturer's instructions.

4 Thread the prong of the buckle through this eyelet, making sure that buckle is lying on the right side of the belt. Turn back the short end and overcast it neatly to the wrong side o belt.

5 Measure from the prong to the oth end of the belt and mark positions for several eyelet holes, placing them abc 1in (2.5cm) apart.

6 Insert the eyelets as before. To ma them really secure, first apply a small patch of iron-on interfacing to the und side of the belt.

*Making a tassel
*Braided tie with tassels
*Inserting godets
*Overlaid seam
*Pattern for a flamenco skirt:
 adapting the pattern;
 directions for making

king a tassel

advantages of making your own
els instead of buying them is that
can be made to match the color of a
ent and can be made in the size
material you choose.

1 Cut a piece of cardboard the desired
length of the tassel. Wind the yarn around
the cardboard until it is thick enough to
make the tassel. Tie the loops at the top
of the card with a length of yarn
threaded through a needle

2 Cut through the lower loops and remove
the card. Fold the threads back over the
knot and bind them with yarn $\frac{5}{8}$in (1.5cm)
from the top. Slip needle under binding
and bring it out at the top. Leave enough
thread at the top to attach tassel.

ided tie with tassels

d or knitting yarn can be used to
e a braided tie. The thickness of the
d will vary according to that of the
used. If you want to attach tassels
e ends, the size of the braid should
proportion to the size of the tassels.

1 For one tie, cut three lengths of cord
or yarn from each color to the length
required for the tie, plus one-third extra,
because when the lengths are braided,
the tie will be shorter. Pin or baste all the
strands together at one end, and secure
them in a closed drawer or around the
back of a chair. Braid the cord by bringing
one layer over another in rotation.

2 When braid is complete, sew the ends of
the cord together. Attach a tassel to each
end and work in the ends of the braid.

Simon Butcher

73

Inserting godets

Godets are triangular pieces of fabric which are set into garments to give added width or flare, usually at a hem edge. Made in a contrasting fabric, as on the skirt, opposite, they will give a decorative effect, as well as adding fullness. The godets may be cut on the straight grain, but if they are cut on the bias, they will add a pretty "swing" to a skirt. Godets can be set into a seam, inserted between the gores of a skirt or set into a slit opening. The skirt shown opposite has godets inserted between the gores.

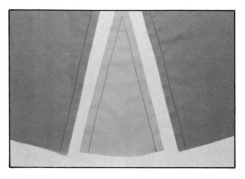

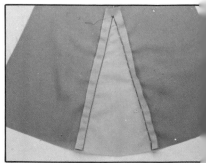

1 When inserting a godet between two gores, or other main sections of a garment, staystitch the seam edges of the godet and of the two gores. With right sides together and raw edges matching, pin one side of godet to adjacent section.

2 Baste and stitch this seam, from the lower edge up to the center point of the godet ⅝in (1.5cm) from the top. Stitch the other side of the godet to the adjacent section in the same way forming a point at the top.

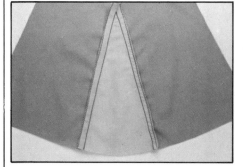

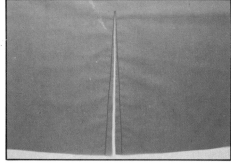

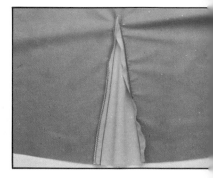

3 Finish the seams by overcasting together, or use zig-zag stitch. Remove basting and press seams away from the godet.

4 When inserting the godet into a slit opening, staystitch the seam edges as before. Before cutting the slit opening on the garment, reinforce it with staystitching, taking the full seam allowance at the bottom and tapering to nothing just above the slit mark. Slash along the line, almost to the stay-stitching at the top.

5 With right sides together, pin the godet into the opening, matching the seamlines of the godet accurately to staystitching of the opening. The seam allowance of the opening will taper to almost nothing at the point, so that the godet will lie flat at the top. Baste along the seamlines. Stitch the seams, taking only one stitch across the point. Finish seams together and press them away from the godet.

Overlaid seam

This seam technique is very useful if the pieces to be joined are cut on the bias and might stretch if they are stitched with a plain seam (as on the skirt shown opposite), or if the overlying section is to be joined to a gathered piece. In the latter case the under section is gathered to fit the upper piece before the seam is completed by the following method.

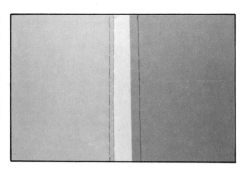

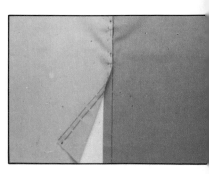

1 Mark the seamlines of both pieces with lines of basting. Fold down the seam allowance of the overlying section to the wrong side on the seamline. Baste and press in place.

2 After joining any necessary pieces (as side seams), overlay the top section onto the bottom piece, matching the seamlines. Pin it in place.

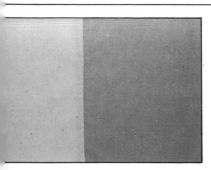

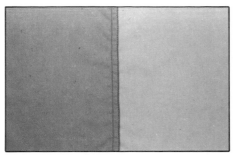

orking from the right side, baste and
h through all thicknesses close to
olded edge. Remove basting and
s.

4 On the wrong side, finish the seam
allowances together with overcasting
or zig-zag stitch and press them
upward.

5 If you wish, the overcasting can be
omitted and a second row of stitching
added, $\frac{1}{4}$in (5mm) from the first, on the
right side. This is a good method to use if
the under-section is gathered.

amenco skirt

nce the light fantastic in
Spanish-inspired skirt. The
trasting godets and belt
ke a simple garment some-
g special.

Adapting the pattern
Measurements
The skirt is made by adapting the pattern
for the basic skirt from the Stitch by
Stitch Pattern Pack, available in sizes
10 to 20, which correspond to sizes
8 to 18 in ready-made clothes.

Materials
3 sheets of tracing paper 35 × 40in
(90 × 100cm)
Flexible curve
Yardstick, right triangle

Skirt

1 For the front pattern, trace the whole of the basic skirt front as shown. Mark the hemline and mark a point on each side on the hemline 2in (5cm) in from the side cutting lines.

2 Re-draw the side cutting lines from these marks and taper them into the original cutting lines at hip level. Mark the side seam allowances ⅝in (1.5cm) from the new cutting lines.

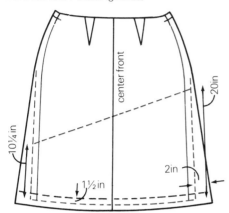

3 To mark the top section of the skirt front, measure 20in (51cm) up the left side seamline from the new hem edge and mark. Measure 10¼in (26cm) up the right side seamline and mark. Draw a line across the pattern to connect these two marks as shown.

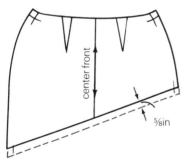

4 Cut along this line to separate the pattern. Add ⅝in (1.5cm) seam allowance to bottom edge of top section. Mark the grain line on the center front.

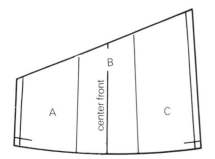

5 Measuring between the side seamlines on the lower skirt section, divide this piece into three equal parts. Draw two lines to indicate the three sections. From the left side, label them A, B, C. The lines will not be parallel to the center front as the skirt is slightly flared.

6 Cut along the two lines to separate the three sections. Begin with piece C and draw a line through the center of this section. To add flare, cut along the center line, but do not cut through the pattern at the top edge. Spread the pattern out by 2¼in (6cm) at lower edge. Insert and tape paper behind the slash. Straighten the angle of the top line as shown. Add ⅝in (1.5cm) seam allowance to top edge and inner side edge.

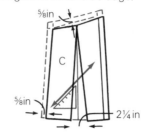

7 To mark the grain line, draw a line through the center of the pattern piece and, using a right triangle placed at a right angle to this line, mark bias on the true as shown.

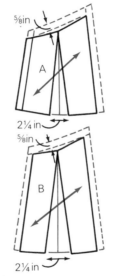

8 Repeat these measurements and directions for the other two sections, adding ⅝in (1.5cm) seam allowances to top and **both** side edges of section B, and the top and inner side edge of section A.

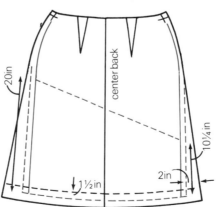

9 For the back pattern, trace the whole basic skirt back pattern as shown.

Follow the directions and measureme[nts] given for altering the front pattern, bu[t] make sure that the line separating the top and bottom sections of the skirt s[...] in the opposite direction.

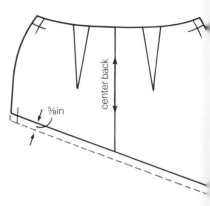

10 Cut along this line to separate the two sections. Add ⅝in (1.5cm) seam allowance to the bottom edge of the t[op] section. Mark the grain line along the center back.

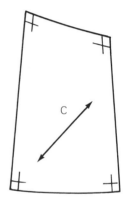

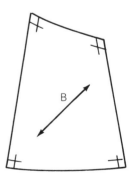

11 Divide the bottom section of the skirt back into three equal parts using the same measurements and directio[ns] as given for the front.

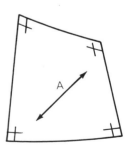

Belinda

Godets and belt

There are two godets in the skirt front, two in the skirt back and one at each side seam, making six godets altogether. Working from the left side seam to the right side seam, number the godets 1, 2, 3, 4. Numbers 1 and 4 are cut once each and numbers 2 and 3 are cut twice each (for front **and** back). Begin making the pattern for number 1. (All godet pieces are labeled G in cutting layout).

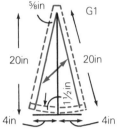

1 Draw two guidelines forming an inverted "T" shape. Mark the length of the godet along center line, 20in (51cm) up from bottom edge. This is the length of left side seam of bottom section of skirt.
2 At the lower edge of the T, mark 4in (10cm) out from each side of the center point. Connect these marks at the top of the T to make a triangle. Measure 20in (51cm) down the sides of the triangle and mark. Using a flexible curve, re-draw the bottom of the godet as shown.
3 Add ⅝in (1.5cm) seam allowance to top and side edges of godet and mark a 1½in (4cm) hem allowance. Using a right triangle placed against the center line, mark the grain line on the bias.

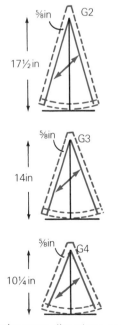

4 Using the same directions as for first godet, make patterns for other godets to following measurements: No. 2: 17½in (44cm); No. 3: 14in (36cm); No. 4: 10¼in (26cm). Mark grain line on each piece on bias as before.

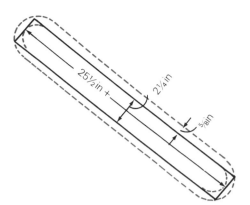

5 To make the belt pattern, draw a rectangle to the length of the waist (pulled fairly closely) 2¼in (6cm) wide. Using a flexible curve, shape both ends as shown. Add ⅝in (1.5cm) seam allowance to all edges. Mark a grain line at a right angle to one long edge.

Directions for making

Suggested fabrics
Linen, rayon, twill, poplin, seersucker.

Materials
Skirt
36in (90cm)-wide fabric without nap:
    Sizes 10, 12: 2⅜yd (2.2m)
    Sizes 14, 16: 2⅝yd (2.4m)
    Sizes 18, 20: 2⅞yd (2.6m)
Godets and belt
36in (90cm)-wide contrasting fabric without nap:
    Sizes 10, 12: 1½yd (1.3m)
    Sizes 14, 16: 1⅝yd (1.4m)
    Sizes 18, 20: 1¾yd (1.5m)
36in (90cm)-wide interfacing: for all sizes: ¼yd (.2m) (for sizes 18, 20 join interfacing at center back)
Matching thread
8in (20cm) skirt zipper
Hook and eye
Two large eyelets (optional)
3⅜yd (3m) cord or similar materials for tie and tassels (will depend on thickness of cord)

Key to adapted pattern pieces
Bottom skirt front

Gore **A**	Cut 1
Gore **B**	Cut 1
Gore **C**	Cut 1
Bottom skirt back	
Gore **A2**	Cut 1
Gore **B2**	Cut 1
Gore **C2**	Cut 1
D Top skirt front	Cut 1
E Top skirt back	Cut 1
F Waistband	Cut 1
G Godet 1	Cut 1
2	Cut 2
3	Cut 2
4	Cut 1
H Belt	Cut 2

Interfacing use pieces **F** Cut 1 to half width only; **H** Cut 1

1 With right sides together, fold, baste and stitch the front and back waist darts. Press darts toward the center. Staystitch all around the lower edges of the skirt sections to prevent stretching.
2 With right sides together, baste and stitch the side seams of the top section of the skirt, leaving an opening for zipper in the left side seam. Finish and press seams open. Insert zipper into the opening as shown in Volume 2, pages 44 and 45.

3 Staystitch across the top edges of the lower sections of the skirt. Insert the six godets as directed on page 74. setting the longest godet into the left side seam, and the shortest into right side seam. The sequence (clockwise) will be G1, C, G2, B, G3, A, G4, A2, G3 B2, G2, C2 and back to G1. Overcast seams together; press away from godet

4 Matching side godets with side seam baste and stitch the skirt top to the skirt bottom using the overlaid seam method (see page 74).

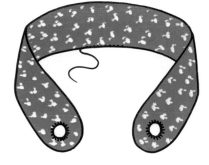

Terry Evans

9 Turn belt right side out through the opening and baste around the edges. Press. Turn in the seam allowances at the opening and slip stitch the edges together. Press. Topstitch $\frac{1}{4}$in (5mm) from the outer edges if desired. Complete with metal or handworked eyelets at each end (see Volume 18, page 77). Eyelets must be large enough to take the braided tie.

10 Make tie and tassels as shown on page 73. Or, omit the braided tie and tassels and insert a ribbon or lacing that matches or coordinates with the main fabric.

epare the waistband and attach to kirt as directed in Volume 3, page 65. plete the waistband with skirt hook eye.

this stage, let the skirt hang on a ger for at least two days so the fabric drop to its final level. Straighten the er edge of the skirt as shown in Volume page 62 and turn up the hem using the t suitable method for the fabric being . A 1$\frac{1}{2}$in (4cm) hem allowance has n included; this can be trimmed to a ower width if required.

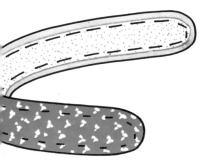

m away the seam allowance around dges of the belt interfacing. Baste nterfacing to the wrong side of one piece.

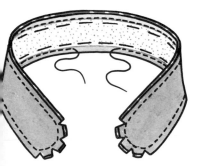

ith right sides together, baste and :h the two belt pieces together, ng a $\frac{5}{8}$in (1.5cm) seam, leaving 6in cm) open along one edge. Trim seam wances to $\frac{1}{4}$in (5mm). Clip curves.

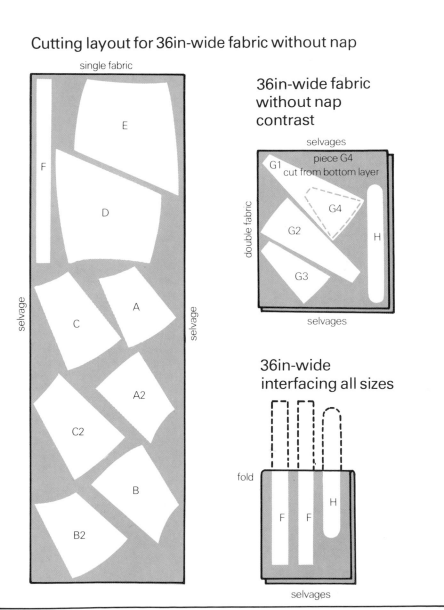

Cutting layout for 36in-wide fabric without nap

single fabric

F
E
D
C
A
A2
C2
B
B2

36in-wide fabric without nap contrast

selvages

G1
piece G4 cut from bottom layer
G4
G2
G3
H

double fabric

selvages

36in-wide interfacing all sizes

fold

F
F
H

selvages

John Hutchinson

Well built

Lay firm foundations for go
looks with this stunning bla
and white jacket and pullov
The brick pattern is fun
crochet and grows fast—
start building today.

Sizes

To fit 34-36[38-40]in (87-92[97-102] cm) bust/chest.
Jacket Length, 18½[19½]in (47[50]cm). Sleeve seam, 15¾in (40cm).
Pullover Length, 27½[28½]in (70[72]cm). Sleeve seam, 20in (51cm).
Note Directions for larger size are in brackets []; if there is only one set of figures it applies to both sizes.

Materials

Jacket 18[22]oz (500[600]g) of a knitting worsted in white
9[11]oz (250[300]g) in black
Pullover 23[27]oz (650[750]g) in white
13[15]oz (350[400]g) in black
Size G (4.50mm) crochet hook
1 pair No. 7 (5mm) knitting needles

Gauge

15sts and 10 rows to 4in (10cm) in patt worked on size G (4.50mm) hook.
Note Wind black yarn into smaller balls (approx 3 balls from each 2oz [50g] ball) and use a separate ball of black for each vertical stripe.

Jacket

Main part

Using size G (4.50mm) hook and white, make 139[159]ch.
Base row 1sc into 2nd ch from hook, 1sc into each ch to end. Turn.
Beg patt.
1st row (RS) With white, work 3ch to count as first dc, 1dc into each of next 11[13] sts leaving last 2 loops of last dc on hook, *draw one ball of black through 2 loops on hook to complete dc, then work 1dc into each of next 2 sts leaving last 2 loops of 2nd dc on hook, draw white through 2 loops on hook, then work 1dc into each of next 12[14] sts leaving last 2 loops of last dc on hook, rep from * to end, completing last dc of last rep in normal way. Turn.
2nd row With white, work 3ch, 1dc into each of next 11[13]dc leaving last 2 loops of last dc on hook, *bring white to front of work, draw black through 2 loops on hook, then work 1dc into each of next 2dc leaving last 2 loops of 2nd dc on hook, bring black to front of work, draw white

through 2 loops on hook, then work 1dc into each of next 12[14]dc leaving last 2 loops of last dc on hook, rep from * to end, completing last dc of last rep in normal way. Turn.
3rd and 4th rows As first and 2nd.
5th row With black, work 2ch, 1hdc into each st to end. Turn.
6th row With black, work 1ch, 1sc into each st to within last 2ch. Turn.
7th row With white, work 3ch, 1dc into each of next 4[5] sts leaving last 2 loops of last dc on hook, *draw black through last 2 loops, 1dc into each of next 2 sts leaving last 2 loops of 2nd dc on hook, draw white through 2 loops on hook, then work 1dc into each of next 12[14] sts leaving last 2 loops of last dc on hook, rep from * to end, finishing last rep with 5[6]dc in white.
8th row With white, work 3ch, 1dc into each of next 4[5]dc leaving last 2 loops of last dc on hook, *bring white to front of work, draw black through 2 loops on hook, then work 1dc into each of next 2dc leaving last 2 loops of 2nd dc on hook, bring black to front of work, draw white through 2 loops on hook, then work 1dc into each of next 12[14]dc leaving last 2 loops of last dc on hook, rep from * to end, finishing last rep with 5[6]dc in white.
9th and 10th rows As 7th and 8th.
11th and 12th rows As 5th and 6th.
These 12 rows form patt.
Cont in patt until work measures 9in (23cm); end with a WS row.

Divide for armholes

Next row Patt over first 33[38] sts, sl st over 3 sts for right armhole, 3ch, patt over next 67[77] sts, sl st over next 3 sts for left armhole, 3ch, patt over next 32[37] sts. Turn.
Work on last set of sts for left front.
Cont in patt until work measures 13¾[15] in (35[38]cm); end with a WS row.
Shape neck
Next row Patt to within last 9 sts, turn.
Dec one st at neck edge (by working 2 sts tog) on next 3 rows. 21[26] sts. Cont straight until work measures 17[18]in (43[46]cm). Fasten off.
With WS facing rejoin yarn to center sts for back and cont in patt until back is same length as left front. Fasten off. With WS facing rejoin yarn to last set of sts for right

front and cont in patt until work measu 13¾[15]in (35[38]cm); end with a WS row.

Shape neck

Next row Sl st over first 10 sts, patt to e Turn.
Dec one st at neck edge on next 3 rows 21[26] sts. Cont straight until work measures 17[18]in (43[46]cm). Faste off.

Sleeves

Using size G (4.50mm) hook and white make 55[63]ch.
Base row 1sc into 2nd ch from hook, 1sc into each ch to end. Turn.
Cont in patt as for main part, inc one st at each end of every 6th row until there are 62[70] sts, working extra sts into pa Cont straight until 3 complete patt reps have been worked. Fasten off.

Cuffs

With RS facing and using No. 7 (5mm) needles and white, pick up and K 74[82 sts along lower edge of sleeve.
1st ribbing row P2, (K2, P2) to end.
2nd ribbing row K2, (P2, K2) to end.
Rep these 2 rows 3 times more. Bind of in ribbing.

Lower border

With RS facing, using No. 7 (5mm) needles and white pick up and K 186 [210] sts evenly along lower edge. Wo 2 ribbing rows of cuff 4 times. Bind off i ribbing.

Neckband

Join shoulder seams. With RS facing, using No. 7 (5mm) needles and white pick up and K 98 sts evenly around nec edge. Work 2 ribbing rows of cuff 4 tim Bind off in ribbing.

Front bands (alike)

With RS facing, using No. 7 (5mm) needles and white pick up and K 90[94 sts evenly along front edge, including lower border and neckband. Work 2 ribbing rows of cuff 4 times. Bind off in ribbing.

To finish

Do not press. Sew in sleeves, then join sleeve seams. Press seams lightly.

Pullover

Back

Using size G (4.50mm) hook and white, make 69[79]ch.
Base row 1sc into 2nd ch from hook, 1sc into each ch to end. Turn.
Cont in patt as for jacket until work measures 23½[24½]in (60[62]cm). Fasten off.

Front

Work as for back until work measures 12½[13½]in (32[34]cm); end with a WS row.

Divide for neck

Next row Patt over first 33[38] sts, turn. Complete this side of neck first.
Keeping patt correct, dec one st at neck edge on every row—excluding 6th and 12th patt rows (i.e. sc rows worked in black)—until 22[26] sts rem. Cont straight until work measures 23½[24½]in (60[62] cm). Fasten off. With WS facing, skip center 2 sts, rejoin yarn to next st, 3ch, patt to end. Complete to match first side.

Sleeves

Using size G (4.50mm) hook and white,

make 55[63]ch.
Base row 1sc into 2nd ch from hook, 1sc into each ch to end. Turn.
Cont in patt as for main part of jacket, one st at each end of every 6th row un[til] there are 62[70] sts, working extra sts into patt. Cont straight until 3 comple[te] patts and 6 rows have been complete[d] Fasten off.

Cuffs

With RS facing, using No. 7 (5mm) needles and white, pick up and K 54[6] sts evenly along lower edge of sleeve.
Next row P2 tog, (P2, P2 tog) to end. 40[46] sts.
Work in K2, P2 ribbing for 3½in (9cm) beg 2nd row P2 for 2nd size only. Bin[d] off in ribbing.

Waistbands (alike)

With RS facing, using No. 7 (5mm) needles and white, pick up and K 70[7] sts evenly along lower edge. Work 2 ribbing rows of jacket for 4in (10cm). Bind off in ribbing.

Neckband

Join right shoulder seam. With RS facing and using No. 7 (5mm) needles pick up and K 68 sts along left front ne[ck] 2 sts from center front, 68 sts along rig[ht] front neck and 40[44] sts across back neck. 178[182] sts.
Work first ribbing row of jacket cuff.
Next row Rib to within 2 sts of 2 cente[r] front sts, sl 1, K1, psso, K2, K2 tog, rib to end.
Next row Rib to within 2 sts of 2 cente[r] front sts, P2 tog, P2, P2 tog tbl, rib to e[nd] Rep last 2 rows twice more, then work first of these 2 rows again. Bind off in ribbing, dec each side of center sts as before.

To finish

Do not press. Join left shoulder and neckband seam. Mark depth of armhol[e] 8¼[9¼]in (20[23]cm) from shoulder seams on back and front. Sew sleeves [to] armholes between markers, then join s[ide] and sleeve seams. Press seams lightly.

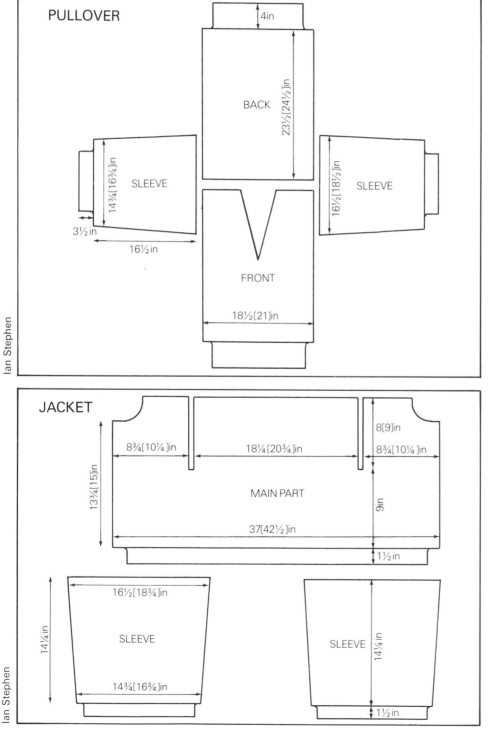

PULLOVER

- 4in
- BACK
- 23½[24½]in
- SLEEVE
- 14¾[16¾]in
- 3½in
- 16½in
- 16½[18½]in
- SLEEVE
- FRONT
- 18½[21]in

JACKET

- 8[9]in
- 8¾[10¼]in
- 18¼[20¾]in
- 8¾[10¼]in
- 13¾[15]in
- MAIN PART
- 37[42½]in
- 9in
- 1½in
- 16½[18¾]in
- SLEEVE
- 14¼in
- 14¾[16¾]in
- SLEEVE
- 14¼in
- 1½in
- 1½in

EXTRA SPECIAL CROCHET

Perfect for parties — child's top is worked in a geometric block-diamond pattern, emphasized on the front with woven ribbon.

boned top

CHART A

× ONE BLOCK
ONE SPACE

1st and 2nd Size
3rd Size

CHART B

7
5
3
1

6
4
2

7
5
3
1

1st Size
2nd Size
3rd Size

Sizes

To fit 20½[23½:25½]in (55[60:65]cm) chest.
Length, 17½[18¾:20]in (44[46:50]cm).
Sleeve seam, (with cuff turned back) 5½[5:5¾]in (13[12:14]cm).
Note Directions for the larger sizes are in brackets []; where there is only one set of figures it applies to all sizes.

Materials

6[6:7]oz (150[150:200]g) of fingering weight yarn
Approx 2yd (2m) of ⅜ (9mm)-wide double-faced satin ribbon
Size E (3.50mm) crochet hook

Gauge

10 sps and 13 rows to 4in (10cm) in filet mesh patt on size E (3.50mm) hook.

Note Sleeves are worked in one piece with both the back and the front.

Back

Using size E (3.50mm) hook, chain 98 [104:110].
Base row 1dc into 8th ch from hook, (2ch, skip next 2ch, 1dc into next ch) 30[32:34] times. Turn. 31[33:35] sps.
Next row 5ch, skip first dc, 1dc into next dc, (2ch, 1dc into next dc) 2[3:4] times, 2dc into next 2ch sp, 1dc into next dc — block formed — *(2ch, 1dc into next dc) 5 times, 2dc into next 2ch sp, 1dc into next dc, rep from * 3 times more, (2ch,

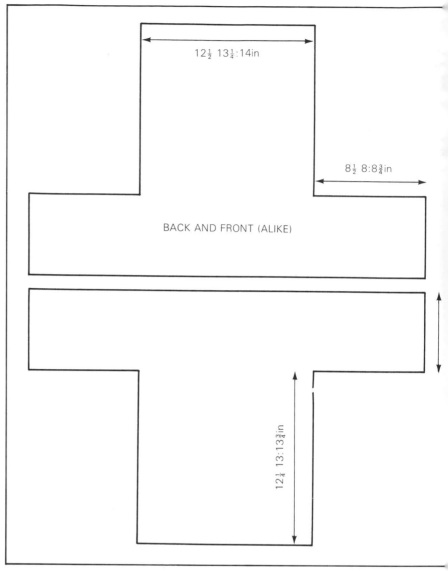

12½ 13¼:14in

8½ 8:8¾in

BACK AND FRONT (ALIKE)

12¼ 13:13¾in

1dc into next dc) 3[4:5] times, working last dc into sp formed by turning ch. Turn.
**Beg with 2nd row, work rem 6 rows of filet diamond patt from chart A.
Work mesh patt row 4[5:6] times.
Work first row of chart A.**
Rep from ** to ** twice more.
Work 2nd and 3rd rows of Chart A, so that 40[42:45] rows have been worked from beg.

Shape sleeves

Next row Chain 65[62:68], 1dc into 4th ch from hook, 1dc into next ch — first block formed —, cont working 4th row of chart B to other side edge, remove hook from loop, join a separate length of yarn to base of last dc worked, chain 62[59:65] and fasten off, return to main yarn and cont working 4th row of chart B across foundation ch just made. Turn.
Work 5th-7th rows of chart B.
Work mesh patt row 4[5:6] times.
Work first-7th rows of chart B.
Work mesh patt row 2[3:3] times.
Fasten off.

Front

Work as given for back.

To finish

Join shoulder seams, leaving centre 23[23:27] sps for neck open.
Ribbon weaving
Beg at right hand edge, weave ribbon through sps above and below block diamond patt on front and backs as shown in photo, twisting ribbon at corners as necessary.
Join side and sleeve seams, reversing seam for 3in (8cm) at cuff edge and enclosing ribbon within side seams.
Lower edging
With RS facing and using size E (3.50mm) hook, join yarn to lower edge at a side seam.
1st round 1ch, 2sc into each sp to end, sl st to first ch.
2nd round 1ch, skip first sc, work in crab st (sc worked from left to right) to end, sl st to first ch.
Fasten off.
Turn back cuffs twice — 1½in (4cm) — and catch to sleeve seam if necessar

KNITTING

ght as air

A classic jacket takes on a completely different look with a multi-layered collar. The jacket and some of the collars are made of contrasting colors of mohair yarn, and the remaining collars are of pearl cotton.

Vince Loden

Sizes

To fit 34[36:38]in (87[92:97]cm) bust.
Length, 28[28¾:29]in (71[73:74]cm).
Sleeve seam, 17[17:17¾]in (43[43:45]cm).
Note Directions for larger sizes are in brackets []; if there is only one set of figures it applies to all sizes.

Materials

16[18:18]oz (450[500:500]g) of a medium-weight mohair in main color (A)
6oz (150g) in first contrasting color (B)
10[10:12]oz (250:300]g) in 2nd contrasting color (C)
2oz (50g) or 95yd (87m) of No. 5 pearl cotton in 3rd contrasting color (D)
1 pair each Nos. 8, 9 and 10½ (5½, 6 and 7mm) knitting needles
10 buttons
Medium-size crochet hook

Gauge

13 sts and 22 rows to 4in (10cm) in stockinette st worked on No. 9 (6mm) needles.

Back

Using No. 8 (5½mm) needles and C, cast on 63[65:69] sts.

1st row K1, *P1, K1, rep from * to end.
2nd row P1, *K1, P1, rep from * to end.
Rep these 2 rows 7 times more.
Change to No. 9 (6mm) needles.
Cut off C, join on A.
Beg with a K row, cont in stockinette st until work measures 20in (51cm); end with a P row.

Shape raglan armholes
Dec one st at each end of next and every foll 4th row until 57[59:61] sts rem, then at each end of every foll alternate row until 37[41:43] sts rem; end with a K row.
Next row K to mark ruffle line.
Beg with a K row, cont to dec on next and every foll alternate row until 27[29:31] sts rem; end with a K row.
Next row K to mark ruffle line.
Beg with a K row, cont to dec on next and every foll alternate row until 19[21:23] sts rem; end with a P row. Bind off.

Pocket linings (make 2)
Using No. 9 (6mm) needles and A, cast on 18 sts. Beg with a K row, cont in stockinette st for 5½in (14cm); end with a P row. Cut off yarn and leave sts on a spare needle.

Left front

Using No. 8 (5½mm) needles and C, cast

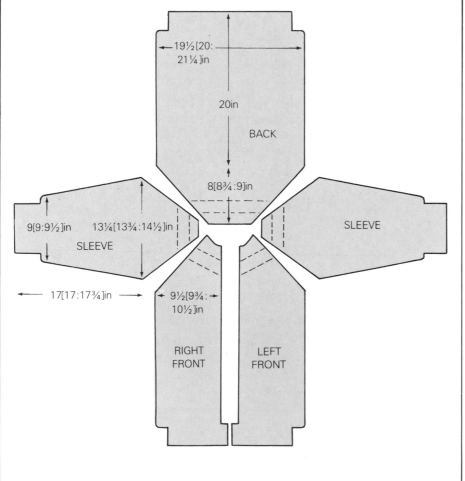

John Hutchinson

on 37[39:41] sts.
1st row K1, *P1, K1, rep from * to end.
2nd row P1, *K1, P1, rep from * to end.
Rep last 2 rows 6 times more, then work first row again.
Next row Rib 7, place these 7 sts on a safety pin, rib to end, for first size only inc one st at end of row. 31[32:34] sts Change to No. 9 (6mm) needles. Cut off C, join on A. Beg with a K row, cont in stockinette st until work measures 8in (20cm); end with a P row.
Pocket row K7[7:8], sl next 18 sts onto a holder and in their place K the sts of one pocket lining, K to end.
Cont in stockinette st until work measures same as back to beg of armhole; end with a P row.
Shape raglan armhole
Dec one st at beg of next row. Work 3 rows without shaping.
2nd and 3rd sizes only
Rep last 4 rows twice more.
All sizes
Dec one st at beg of next and every foll alternate row until 25[28:30] sts rem; end with a P row. Beg ruffle line.
Next row Work 2 tog, K to last 3 sts, P1, K2.
Next row P3, K1, P to end.
Next row Work 2 tog, K to last 5 sts, P1, K4.
Next row P5, K1, P to end.
**Cont in this way, dec one st at armhole edge on every other row and working the "pip" of ruffle line one st nearer to armhole edge on every row until 18[20: 21] sts rem; end with a P row.
Cont to dec one st at armhole edge on next and every foll alternate row, work another ruffle line in the same way, until 14[15:16] sts rem; end at front edge.
Shape neck
Cont to shape armhole and work ruffle line, bind off 4[5:6] sts at beg of next row, then dec one st at neck edge on next and every foll alternate row until 2 sts rem; end with a P row.
Next row Work 2 tog. Fasten off. **

Right front
Using No. 8 (5½mm) needles and C, cast on 37[39:41] sts.
1st row K1, *P1, K1, rep from * to end.
2nd row P1, *K1, P1, rep from * to end.
Rep last 2 rows once [once:twice] more.
1st buttonhole row Rib, 3, bind off 2, rib to end.
2nd buttonhole row Rib to end, casting on 3 sts over those bound off on previous row.
Rib 9[9:7] more rows.
Next row Inc one st on first size only, rib to last 7 sts, turn and leave last 7 sts on a safety pin. 31[32:34] sts. Change to No. 9 (6mm) needles. Cut off C, join on A. Beg with a K row, cont in stockinette st until work measures 8in (20cm); end with a P row.
Pocket row K6[7:8], sl next 18 sts onto

Vince Loden

a holder and in their place K the sts of pocket lining, K to end.
Cont in stockinette st until work measures same as back to beg of armhole; end with a P row.

Shape raglan armhole
Dec one st at end of next row. Work 3 rows without shaping.

2nd and 3rd sizes only
Rep last 4 rows twice more.

All sizes
Dec one st at end of next and every foll alternate row until 25[28:30] sts rem; end with a P row.
Beg ruffle line.
Next row K2, P1, K to last 2 sts, work 2 tog.
Next row P to last 4 sts, K1, P3.
Next row K4, P1, K to last 2 sts, work 2 tog.

Next row P to last 6 sts, K1, P5.
Work as for left front from ** to **.

Sleeves
Using No. 8 (5½mm) needles and C, cast on 29[29:31] sts.
1st row K1, *P1, K1, rep from * to end.
2nd row P1, *K1, P1, rep from * to end.
Rep last 2 rows 8 times more. Change to No. 9 (6mm) needles. Cut off C, join on A. Beg with a K row, cont in stockinette st, inc one st at each end of 3rd[5th:7th] row and every foll 10th[8th:8th] row until there are 43[45:47] sts. Cont straight until work measures 17[17:17¾]in (43 [43:45]cm); end with a P row.

Shape raglan
Dec one st at each end of next and every foll 4th row until 29[29:31] sts rem; end with a P row.
First and 3rd sizes only: dec one st at each end of next row.
All sizes:

Next row K to mark ruffle line.
Beg with a K row, cont to dec on next and every foll alternate row until 17 sts rem; end with a K row.
Next row K to mark ruffle line.
Beg with a K row, cont to dec on next and every foll alternate row until 9 sts rem; end with a P row. Bind off.

Left front lower ruffle
Using No. 9 (6mm) needles, C and with RS facing, pick up and K 14[16:18] sts from "pips" of lower ruffle line.
Next row (P1, K1) into first st, *(P1, K1, P1) into next st, (K1, P1, K1) into next rep from * to last st, (P1, K1, P1) into last st. 41[47:53] sts. Change to No. 10½ (7mm) needles.
1st row K1, *P1, K1, rep from * to end.
2nd row P1, *K1, P1, rep from * to end.
Rep last 2 rows until ruffle measures 6¾in (17cm); end with a WS row.
Bind off very loosely in ribbing. Work right front lower ruffle in same way.

Lower back ruffle
Using No. 9 (6mm) needles, C and with RS facing, pick up and K 37[41:43] sts across lower back ruffle line.
Next row (WS) (P1, K1, P1) into first st, *(K1, P1, K1) into next st, (P1, K1, P1) into next st, rep from * to end. 111[123:129] sts. Complete as for left front lower ruffle.

Sleeve lower ruffle
Using No. 9 (6mm) needles, D and with RS facing, pick up and K 25[27:27] sts across lower ruffle line.
Next row K twice into every st. 50[54:54] sts.
Cont in garter st until ruffle measures 6¾in (17cm); end with a WS row.
Bind off very loosely.

Second ruffle
Join raglan seams. Using No. 9 (6mm) needles, B and with RS facing, beg at left front and pick up and K 10[11:11] sts across "pips" of upper ruffle line, across 15 sts on sleeve, 25[27:29] sts across back, 15 sts across second sleeve and 10[11:11] sts across "pips" on right front. 75[79:81] sts.
Next row (P1, K1, P1) into first st, *(K1, P1, K1) into next st, (P1, K1, P1) into next st, rep from * to end. 231[237:243] sts.
Change to No. 10½ (7mm) needles. Wo 5in (13cm) as for left front lower ruffle. Bind off very loosely in ribbing.

Left neck ruffle
Using No. 9 (6mm) needles D and with RS facing, beg at back raglan seam and pick up and K 9 sts across top of sleeve and 14[14:16] sts down left side of nec 23[23:25] sts.
Next row K twice into every st. 46[46:50]sts.

row *K twice into next st, K1, rep
* to end. 69[69:75] sts.
in garter st until ruffle measures 4in
m); end with a WS row. Bind off very
ly.

neck ruffle
No. 9 (6mm) needles, D and with
cing, beg at base of neck shaping
ick up and K14[14:16] sts up right
f neck and 9 sts across top of sleeve.
as for left neck ruffle.

No. 9 (6mm) needles and C, cast
[67:76] sts.
row (RS) P to end.
row *K2, K twice into next st, rep
* to last st, K1. 85[89:101] sts.
att, using another separate ball

of C and twisting yarns tog when
changing colors to prevent a hole.
Next row P19 C, 47[51:63] A, 19 C.
Next row K19 C, 47[51:63] A, 19 C.
Rep last 2 rows until work measures 8in
(20cm); end with a P row.
Cut off A and cont in C only.
Next row *K2, K2 tog, rep from * to last
st, K1. 64[67:76] sts. Bind off.

Buttonhole band
Using No. 8 (5½mm) needles, C and with
WS of work facing, join yarn to sts on
right front safety pin.
Cont in ribbing as set, making 9 more
buttonholes at intervals of 2¾in (7cm)
measured from base of previous
buttonhole. Cont in ribbing until band,
when slightly stretched, fits up front;
end with a WS row. Bind off in ribbing.

Button band
Using No. 8 (5½mm) needles, C and with
RS facing, join yarn to sts on left front
safety pin. Work as for buttonhole band,
omitting buttonholes.

Pocket tops
Using No. 8 (5½mm) needles, C and with
RS facing, join yarn to sts on spare
needle. Work 4 rows K1, P1 ribbing.
Bind off.

To finish
Join side and sleeve seams. Sew bands
pocket linings and pocket tops in place.
Fold collar in half and join all around.
Sew collar to neck edge above neck
ruffles. Using A, make 2 crochet chains
about 14in (36cm) long and sew to neck
edge for ties. Sew on buttons.

chnique tip Working ruffles

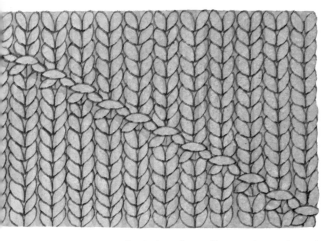

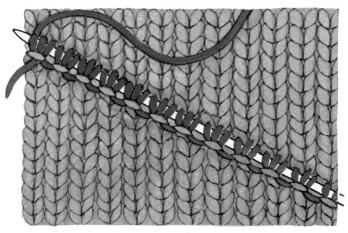

make the picking up of stitches for ruffles easier, a line of
'' is formed by working a purl stitch on the right side and a
titch on the wrong side of the main fabric.

3 Join on yarn for ruffle and knit stitches in the usual way.
To give the ruffle extra width, work increases all along the next
row. We have worked three times into each stitch.

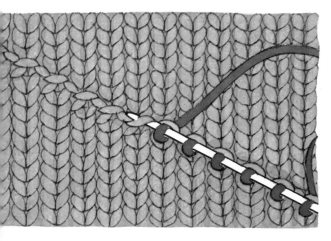

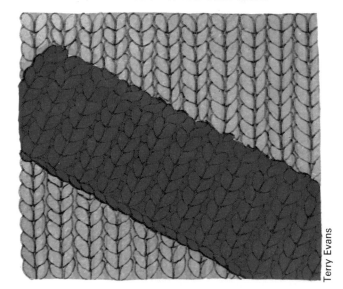

Terry Evans

e pip section where you want the ruffle to hang should be
e top when picking up stitches so that the pips will be
neath the ruffle. To pick up the stitches for the ruffle, insert
eedle into the pip.

4 Work the required depth for the ruffle, then bind off. The
ruffle lies in a neat line on the fabric.

EXTRA SPECIAL KNITTING

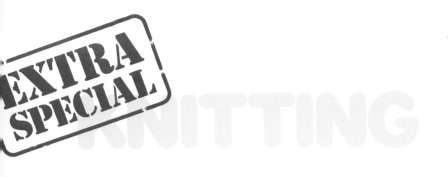

Jigsaw puzzle pattern

Don't be confused. Follow the chart and add a puzzle pattern to a classic crewneck sweater.

29[31:33:35:37]in (74[79:84:89:
n) bust.
th, 19½[20:20½:21:21]in (49[50:
2:52]cm).
e seam, 17[17¼:18:18:18]in
44:46:46:46]cm).
Directions for larger sizes are in
cets []; if there is only one set of
es it applies to all sizes.

rials

[14:14:16:18]oz (350[400:400:450:500]g) of a sport yarn in main color (A)
z (25g) in each of 5 contrasting colors (B, C, D, E and F)
pair each Nos. 3 and 6 (3¼ and 4½mm) knitting needles

ge

s and 30 rows to 4in (10cm) in
kinette st on No. 6 (4mm) needles.

When working patt from chart do
carry colors across WS of work, but
separate balls as required, twisting
s when changing color to avoid
ng a hole.

t

g No. 3 (3¼mm) needles and A, cast
4[80:84:90:96] sts.
k 15 rows K1, P1, ribbing.
ow Rib 1[4:1:4:8], (pick up loop
g between needles and work into back
– called make 1 or M1 –, rib
9:9:9] sts) 9 times, M1, rib 1[4:2:
. 84[90:94:100:106] sts.
nge to No. 6 (4½mm) needles.
ding RS rows from right to left and
rows from left to right, work rows 1 to
from chart on page 92.
t in patt from chart, shape neck as foll:
t row Patt 34[36:37:39:41], turn
leave rem sts on a spare needle.
nplete this side of neck first. Dec one
neck edge on next 5 rows. Work 1
. Now dec one st at neck edge on
t and foll alternate rows. 27[29:30:32:
sts.
k 10[14:16:20:20] rows without
ping. Bind off.
urn to sts on spare needle. With RS
ng, place center 16[18:20:22:24] sts
holder, rejoin yarn to next st and work
nd of row. Complete to match first
side, reversing shaping.

Back

As front, omitting neck shaping.

Sleeves

Using No. 3 (3¼mm) needles and A, cast on 37[37:39:41:43] sts.
1st row K1, (P1, K1) to end.
2nd row P1, (K1, P1) to end.
Rep these 2 rows 6 times more, then work the first row again.
Inc row Rib 2[2:3:4:5], (M1, rib 8) 4 times, M1, rib 3[3:4:5:6]. 42[42:44:46:48] sts.
Change to No. 6 (4½mm) needles. Beg with a K row, cont in stockinette st inc one st at each end of first[first:9th:first:9th] row and every foll 6th[6th:5th:6th:5th] row until there are 78[78:84:84:88] sts. Cont straight until work measures 17[17¼:18:18:18]in (43[44:46:46:46] cm); end with a P row. Bind off.

Neckband

Join right shoulder seam. With RS facing join yarn to left front shoulder and using No. 3 (3¼mm) needles and A, pick up and K 14[16:18:20:22] sts down left front neck, K sts from holder, pick up and K 14[16:18:20:22] sts from right front neck and 28[30:32:34:36] sts across back neck. 72[80:88:96:104] sts.
Ribbing row (K1, P1) rep from * to end.
Rep ribbing row for 2[2:2:2¼:2¼:2¼]in (5[5:5:6:6]cm). Bind off in ribbing.

To finish

Join left shoulder and neckband seam. Mark depth of armholes 7[7:7½:7½:8]in (18[18:19:19:20.5]cm) from shoulder seams on back and front. Sew sleeves to armholes, join side and sleeve seams. Fold neckband to WS and slip stitch in place.

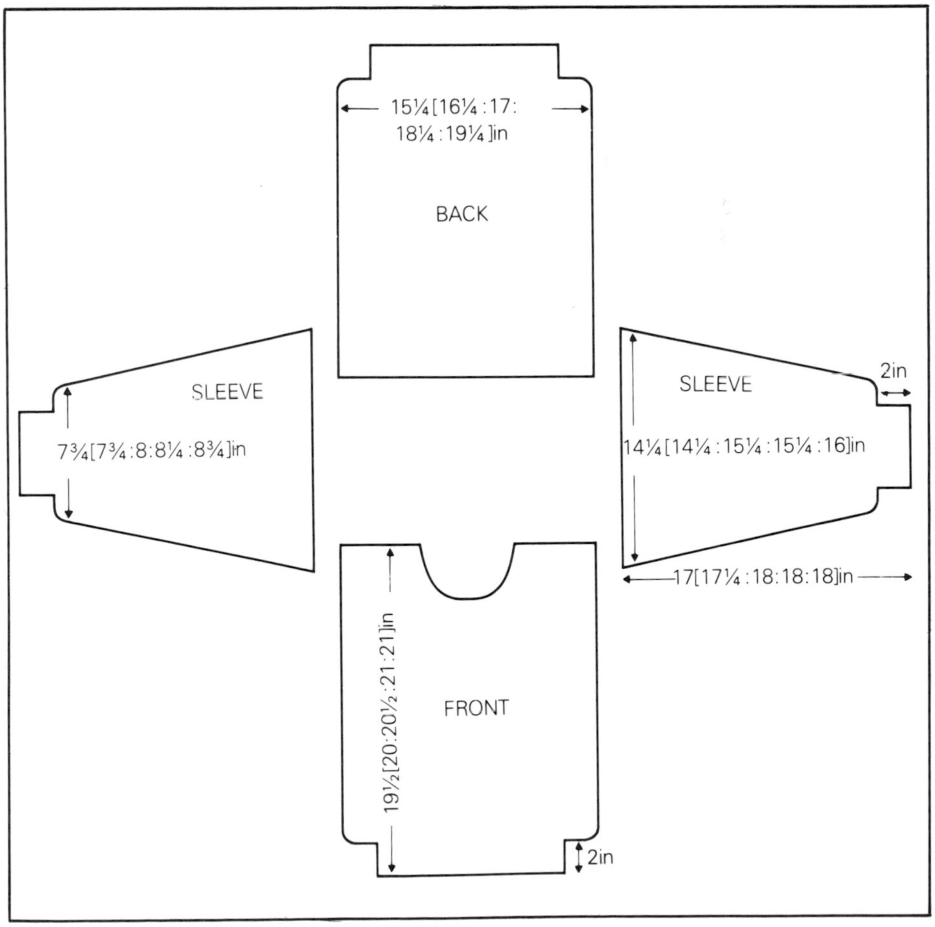

15¼[16¼:17:18¼:19¼]in
BACK
SLEEVE
7¾[7¾:8:8¼:8¾]in
SLEEVE
2in
14¼[14¼:15¼:15¼:16]in
17[17¼:18:18:18]in
19½[20:20½:21:21]in
FRONT
2in

Brian Mayor

ncy pants

These practical overalls for a baby have snaps around the inside of the legs for easy diaper changing.

Measurements

To fit ages 3 to 6 [6 to 12] months.
Waist to ankle length, $15\frac{1}{2}$[$19\frac{1}{4}$]in
(39[49]cm).
Note Measurements are given for the
smaller size. Figures for the larger size are
in brackets []. If only one figure is given,
it applies to both sizes.

Suggested fabrics

Medium-weight cotton.

Materials

$\frac{7}{8}$[$1\frac{3}{4}$]yd (.8[1.5]m) of 36in (90cm)-
  wide fabric or $\frac{7}{8}$[1]yd (.8[.9]m)
  of 45in (115cm)-wide fabric
Matching thread; 6 large snaps
$\frac{1}{4}$yd (.2m) of $\frac{3}{8}$in (1cm)-wide elastic
$4 \times \frac{5}{8}$in (1.5cm)-diameter buttons
$1\frac{3}{4}$yd (1.5m) of $\frac{1}{2}$in (1.3cm)-wide
  bias binding, flexible curve
Yardstick; tailor's chalk

1 Using a yardstick, flexible curve and
tailor's chalk, mark pattern pieces on
fabric, following measurement diagram
and cutting layout. Cut out all pieces
twice. Mark side openings with tailor's
tacks. A $\frac{5}{8}$in (1.5cm) seam allowance and
$\frac{3}{4}$in (2cm) hem are included.

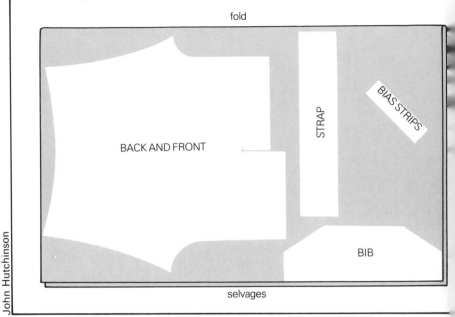

Cutting layout for 45in-wide fabric

fold

STRAP

BIAS STRIPS

BACK AND FRONT

BIB

selvages

John Hutchinson

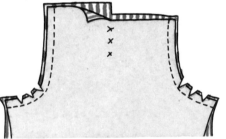

2 With right sides together and raw
edges matching, pin, baste and stitch
back and front seams from waist to
crotch. Clip curves and press seams open.

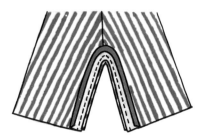

Terry Evans

3 With right sides together and raw edges
matching, pin, baste and stitch binding to
inside leg edges on back and front.

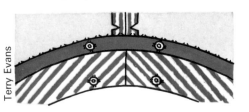

4 Turn bias binding to inside and slip
stitch free edge in place. On front legs,

sew top half of a snap to binding, 1 in
(2.5cm) form each side of the center
seam. Sew two more snaps $2\frac{3}{4}$in (7cm)
apart, down each front leg. Sew the
corresponding halves of snaps to the
right side of back legs.

5 Turn up and sew a $\frac{3}{4}$in (2cm) hem on
each pants leg.

6 Cut two bias strips of fabric, 2in (5cm)
by twice the length of the side opening.
Apply to side openings as described in
Volume 13, page 105, steps 1 to 3.

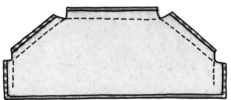

7 With right sides facing, stitch the bib
pieces together, leaving the lower edges

open. Clip the corners. Turn right side
and press.

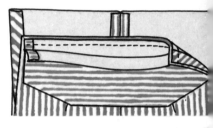

8 Measure $1\frac{3}{4}$[2]in (4.5[5]cm) from
side of center front seam on pants. Pi
and baste a $\frac{1}{4}$in (5mm) pleat on each
With right sides together, pin, baste a
stitch outer layer of bib to pants front

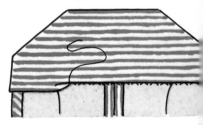

9 Turn in seam allowance on free edg
bib and slip stitch it over stitching lin
turning in side facings so that bib hol
them in place.

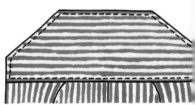

10 Topstitch all around bib, $\frac{1}{4}$in (5mr
from the edges.

11 Cut a length of binding to fit back waist, plus seam allowances. With right sides facing and raw edges matching, stitch binding along back waist edge, turning in ends. Turn binding to inside, turn in free edge and slip stitch in place, catching in facings. Leave ends of binding open. Cut elastic to fit back waist of baby, thread through binding and secure ends.

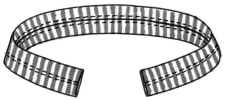

12 Fold straps in half lengthwise, with right sides together, and stitch long edge.

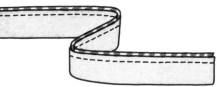

13 Turn straps right side out and press flat, with seam at center of strap. Turn in the ends and baste. Topstitch $\frac{1}{4}$in (5mm) from each side of seam.
14 Stitch straps to back $2\frac{3}{4}[3\frac{1}{4}]$in (7[8]cm) from center back seam on each side. Check length of straps on baby and sew a button at free end of each strap. Sew remaining buttons on the back of the pants, at the top of each side opening.

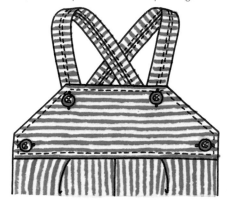

15 Turn overalls right side out and work two $\frac{3}{4}$in (2cm)-long buttonholes on the top edge of the bib and two more buttonholes to correspond with the buttons at the sides.

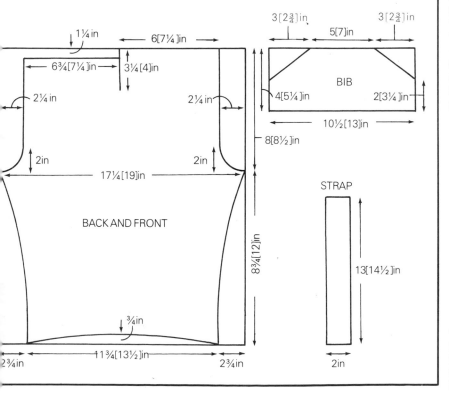

1¼ in

6[7¼]in

6¾[7¼]in

3¼[4]in

2¼ in

2¼ in

2 in

2 in

17¼[19]in

BACK AND FRONT

8¾[12]in

¾ in

11¾[13½]in

2¾ in

2¾ in

3[2¾]in

5[7]in

3[2¾]in

BIB

4[5¼]in

2[3¼]in

10½[13]in

8[8½]in

STRAP

13[14½]in

2 in

SEWING

Hat tricks

Keep a cool head and look great in this flattering summer head-gear. Match your favorite summer outfit with a wide brim to slip over a scarf or a sporty sunshade with interchangeable ties.

Measurements To fit average head s

Suggested fabrics Lightweight cotto

Shady brim

Materials
  1yd (.9m) of 54in (140cm)-wide
    solid color fabric
  1yd (1m) of 54in (140cm)-wide
    contrasting fabric or scarf, 1yd
    (1m) square
  Matching thread; millinery wire
  $\frac{5}{8}$yd (.5m) of 36in (90cm)-wide
    medium-weight non-woven
    interfacing
  $\frac{5}{8}$yd (.5m) of 36in (90cm)-wide
    tarlatan
  $\frac{3}{4}$in (.7m) of 27in (70cm)-wide
    buckram
  Fabric glue; thin string or strong
  Thumbtack; soft pencil; tailor's c

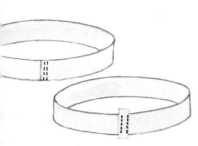

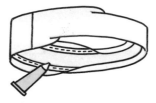

...headband, cut a bias strip of ...am, 1in (2.5cm) wide, by your head ...rement, plus ¾in (2cm) for seams. ...lap the short edges of the strip by ...cm) and sew center back seam with ...nes of backstitch. Cover joining ...arlatan (see Technique tip); press. ...two lengths of millinery wire, each ...cumference of the headband, plus ...cm). Join wire into two circles, ...et stitch to upper and lower edges ...dband and cover wire with tarlatan ...echnique tip).

4 Cut a strip of non-woven interfacing, 1¾in (4.5cm) wide, by circumference of headband. Place interfacing over headband, with short edges to joining and overlapping top and bottom edges by ⅜in (1cm). Turn under overlaps and glue.

5 Cut a bias strip of fabric, 2¾in (7cm)

wide by the circumference of the head-band plus ¾in (2cm). With right sides together and raw edges even, stitch the short edges together, taking ⅜in (1cm) seam allowance. Press seam open.

6 Place fabric headband over buckram headband with right side out, matching seam and overlapping lower edge by ¾in (1cm). Turn overlap to inside of headband and glue in place with fabric glue. Leave the upper edge free for the time being.

Measurement diagram

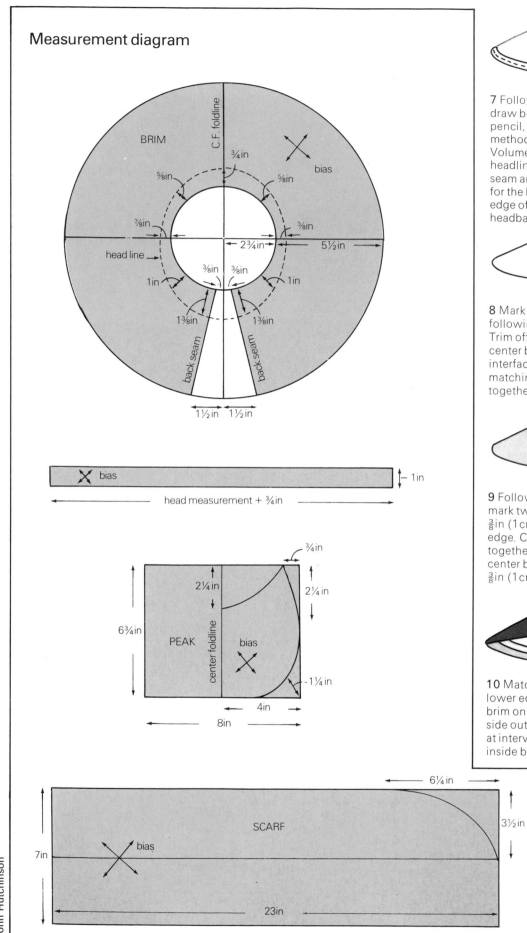

BRIM

C.F. foldline

¾in

bias

⅝in   ⅝in

⅜in   ⅜in

head line

2¾in

5½in

⅜in   ⅜in

1in   1in

1⅜in   1⅜in

back seam   back seam

1½in   1½in

bias   1in

head measurement + ¾in

PEAK

center foldline

¾in

2¼in   2¼in

6¾in

bias

1¼in

4in

8in

SCARF

6¼in

3½in

bias

7in

23in

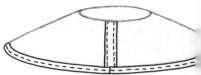

7 Following the measurement diagra[m]
draw brim shape on buckram with a
pencil, using thumbtack and string
method to draw the outer curve (see
Volume 6, page 105). Mark broken li[ne]
headline. Cut out. Join the center bac[k]
seam and cover with tarlatan as descr[ibed]
for the headband. Wire and bind the o[uter]
edge of the brim as described for the
headband.

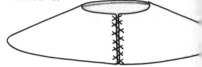

8 Mark and cut the brim in interfacing
following the measurement diagram.
Trim off ⅜in (1cm) seam allowance do[wn]
center back seam edges. Place the
interfacing over the buckram brim,
matching seams. Butt center back ed[ges]
together; herringbone stitch in place.

9 Following the measurement diagra[m]
mark two brim pieces on fabric, addin[g]
⅜in (1cm) seam allowance at the low[er]
edge. Cut out. With right sides togeth[er]
together and raw edges even, stitch
center back seams on both pieces, tak[ing]
⅜in (1cm) allowance. Press seams op[en]

10 Matching seams and overlapping t[he]
lower edge by ⅜in (1cm) place fabric
brim on buckram foundation with righ[t]
side out. Clip into lower seam allowan[ce]
at intervals, turn overlap under and glu[e]
inside brim.

...ace remaining fabric under brim, with
...side out and seams matching. Turn
...r ⅜in (1cm) seam allowance and
...titch in place neatly and as close to
...dge as possible.

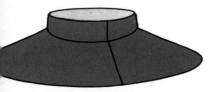

...ip into seam allowance to marked
...line of brim. Place headband over
... matching seams, with finished
... to right side of brim. Press headline
... allowance up into headband, trim
...aste in place. Stab-stitch headband
...m.

...old free edge of fabric over headband,
... under ⅜in (1cm) seam allowance and
...titch in place.

...ut contrasting fabric into a 1yd (1m)
...re and make a narrow rolled hem all
...nd. Tie scarf as shown.

...nshade

...erials
...d (.9m) each of 36in (90cm)-wide
...striped and dotted fabrics
...atching thread; millinery wire
...d (.3m) of 36in (90cm)-wide
...medium-weight non-woven
...interfacing
...d (.5m) of 36in (90cm)-wide tarlatan
...d (.5m) or 27in or (70cm)-wide
...buckram
...oft pencil, tailor's chalk

...llowing the measurement diagram,
... peak shape on buckram with a soft

pencil and cut out. Draw another peak
shape on interfacing and cut out. Wire
curved edge of buckram peak and cover
with tarlatan strip (see Technique tip).
Place interfacing peak on buckram peak.
Baste in place.

2 Following measurement diagram, mark
and cut out two peak shapes from dotted
fabric. With right sides outward, place one
dotted peak on top of interfacing peak
and one dotted peak under buckram.
Baste all layers together.
3 Cut a bias strip of striped fabric,
1½ × 20in (4 × 50cm). Place right side of
strip to right side of peak, with raw edges
matching and sew in place around
curved edge of peak, taking ⅜in (1cm)
seam allowance.
4 Turn under ⅜in (1cm) seam allowance
on free edge of bias strip and slip stitch in
place on underside of peak.
5 Make headband, following steps
1 to 6 of directions for brimmed hat
and using striped fabric.

6 Snip into seam allowance along
straight edge of peak. Place right side of
peak to finished edge of headband,
matching centers, with headband seam
at center back. Baste in place, then stab
stitch. Fold free edge of striped fabric
over headband, turn under ⅜in (1cm)
seam allowance and slip stitch in place.

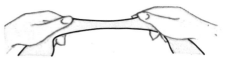

7 Following measurement diagram, mark
and cut out tie piece, half in dotted fabric
and half in striped fabric. Join straight
ends with a French seam. Make a narrow
hem all around. Tie scarf around
headband as shown in photograph.

Technique tips

These millinery methods will help you
make many simple hat styles. Both the
brims shown are made on a foundation
of buckram (a stiffened cotton fabric)
with joinings and edges covered in
tarlatan (a lightly stiffened muslin).
Edges are shaped with millinery wire.

To join millinery wires

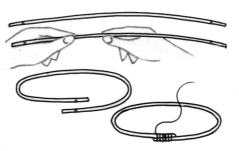

Measure circumference of headband or
brim which is to be wired and add ¾in
(2cm) overlap. Cut off this length of
wire, marking the finished measurement
with a pencil.
Soften the wire by bending it gently
between the fingers and thumbs.
Bend wire around, matching pencil marks
and bind together firmly with sewing
thread.

To wire headband or brim edge

Place wire against edge of buckram brim.
Blanket stitch in place, fastening ends
firmly.

Covering joins in buckram

Cut a ⅝in (1.5cm)-wide bias strip of
tarlatan, to length of seam to be covered.
Hold strip in both hands and stretch the
tarlatan until there is no more "give."
Place on seam and backstitch.

Covering a wired edge

Cut ¾in (2cm)-wide bias strip of tarlatan
and stretch as described above. Fold
in half lengthwise. Place fold over wired
edge and secure with running stitches.

Terry Evans

mmer fun

...ke it one way, in bright
... on material, and it becomes
...cation skirt. If you make it in
...gerie fabric, you have a full-
...th petticoat.

...surements

...sizes 8-10 [12-14].
...th: $43\frac{1}{2}[45\frac{1}{4}]$in (110[115]cm).
...Measurements are given for size 8-
...easurements for the larger size are
...ckets []. If there is only one figure, it
...es to all sizes. A $\frac{5}{8}$in (1.5cm) seam
...ance is included and a $\frac{3}{4}$in (2cm)
...allowance. Check the skirt length
...e cutting out.

...ested fabrics

...or printed cotton; cotton blends;
...ucker; gingham.

...rials

...yd (4m) of 36/45in (90/115cm)-
...wide fabric
...yd (1.5m) of 1in (2.5cm) seam
...binding
...yd (1m) of $\frac{1}{4}$in (5mm) elastic
...d (4.5m) of lace edging (optional)
...ilor's chalk; ruler; flexible curve

...lowing the measurement diagram,
...the skirt sections on fabric, using
...flexible curve and tailor's chalk.
...back and front are alike. Cut out.
...rk and cut out ruffle sections to make
...l length of $4\frac{3}{8}$ [$4\frac{5}{8}$]yd (4 [4.2]m).

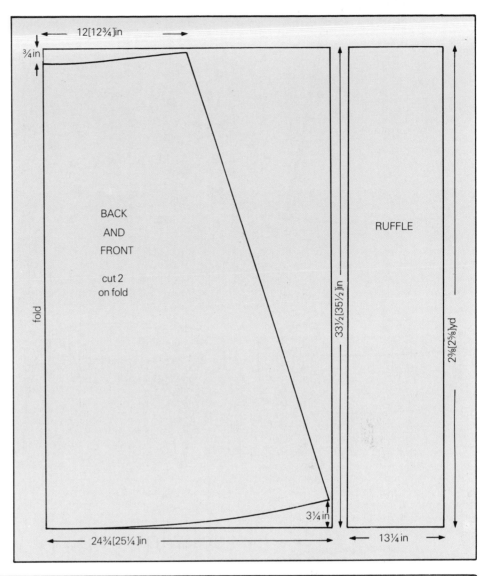

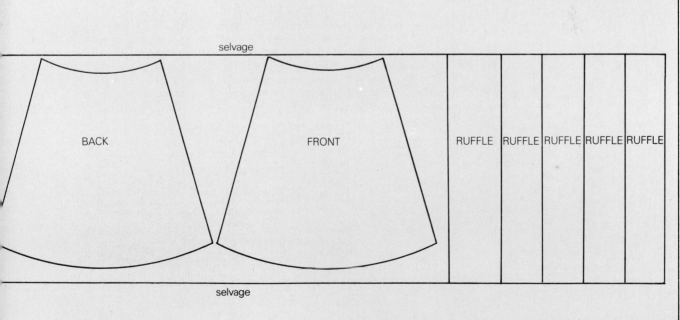

3 With right sides together and raw edges matching, pin, baste and stitch side seams of skirt. Press seams open. Finish lower edge of skirt with zig-zag stitch or overcasting.

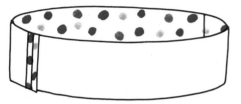

4 With right sides together and raw edges matching, pin, baste and stitch the short seams of the ruffle pieces to make a circle. Press seams open. Finish upper edge of ruffle. Run a line of gathering stitches along the seamline. Pull up gathers until gathering fits lower edge of skirt. Adjust gathers and secure gathering thread.

5 With right sides together and side seams matching, pin, baste and stitch ruffle to lower edge of skirt, working with ruffle on top so as not to crush gathers. Alternately, apply ruffle with heading (see Technique tip).

6 Cut a length of seam binding to fit the top edge of the skirt. Pin, baste and stitch binding to right side of skirt, working along seamline, $\frac{1}{4}$in (5mm) from edge of binding. Turn in ends of binding.

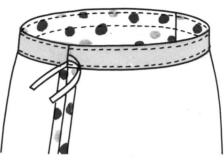

7 Turn seam binding to inside of skirt. Topstitch along free edge of binding and

again $\frac{1}{4}$in (5mm) from waist edge of binding. Thread elastic through chann formed by binding. Pull elastic up to fit waist comfortably and secure ends.

8 Turn up and stitch a $\frac{3}{4}$in (2cm)-deep hem. Add a lace edging if you wish.

Technique tip

Ruffle with gathered heading

This is a pretty way to finish a ruffle around the hem of a skirt or petticoat. The top of the heading can be simply finished with a narrow machine-stitched hem or finished off with machine-embroidered scallops. Another idea is to make the ruffle from eyelet edging with a ready-made scalloped edge.

Make the garment in the usual v turning under and sewing a $\frac{5}{8}$in (1.5c deep hem. Join the ruffle pieces to ma circle, finishing upper and lower edge required.

Run a line of gathers $\frac{3}{4}$-1in (2-2.5 from top edge of ruffle and gather ru to fit hem edge of garment. Then, wrong side of ruffle to right side of ment, position ruffle on hem as sho Topstitch in place over the gathers $\frac{5}{8}$in. (1.5cm) above the hemline of the s

oss-stitched rug

A simple pattern of concentric stripes in vibrant colors makes a rug suited to either modern or traditional decor.

Spike Powell

Working diagram for rug

KEY A – leaf green B – pale pink C – raspberry pink D – ice blue E – peacock blue F – rust G – buttercup

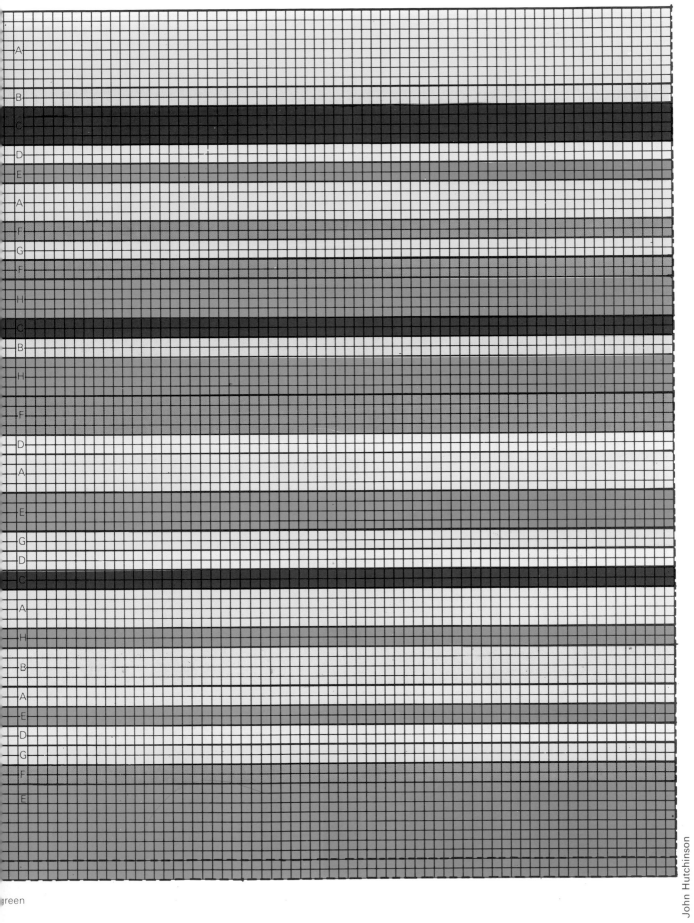

green

Finished size
About 48×28in (122×70cm).

Materials
1½yd (1.3m) of 28in (70cm)-wide rug canvas with 5 holes to 1in (2.5cm)

Rug yarn in the following colors: 15oz (400g) in leaf green; 8oz (200g) in rust; 6oz (150g) in each of kelly green, peacock blue, raspberry pink, ice blue and pale pink; 4oz (100g) in buttercup yellow

No. 13 tapestry needle

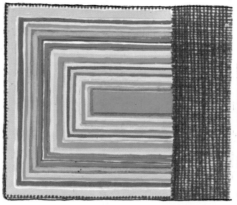

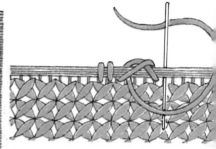

1 Turn under eight threads of canvas along one short edge, folding the canvas along the ninth thread from the raw edge.

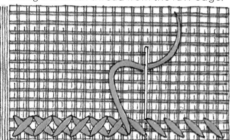

Terry Evans

2 Begin working the rug at the folded short edge, working the first four rows through both layers of the canvas and leaving the thread on the edge unworked. The rug is worked in cross-stitch, with each cross worked over four thread intersections. Make sure that the upper half of each cross slants in the same direction.

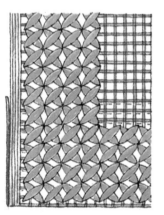

3 Work four rows of leaf green along the whole width of the canvas, then work a few more rows of four stitches along both the long edges to position the design on the canvas.

4 Continue working the design of one quarter of the rug, following the diagram on pages 104-105 for color placement. When one-quarter of the design is completed, you should have 45 stitches across the width of the canvas (including the center stitch marked by the double broken line) and 75 along its length.

5 Complete one half of the rug by reversing the diagram along the horizontal edge marked by the double broken line.

6 Now work the other half of the rug, reversing the diagram both vertically and horizontally.

Leave the last four rows of the design unworked.

7 Count off nine canvas threads, then fold under the canvas along the ninth thread.

Align the mesh carefully and press the fold firmly in place.

8 Work the last four rows through both layers of canvas.

Trim off any surplus canvas that extends beyond the stitching on the underside of the rug.

Janet Allen

9 Work braid stitch in leaf green along both long edges of the rug, working with the wrong side facing. Work a few upright stitches to anchor the thread, then insert the needle in the next hole from back to front; go over the edge and into the fourth hole to the right, back to the second hole, forward to the fifth hole and so on. Finish with two or three upright stitches. Darn thread ends into the work.

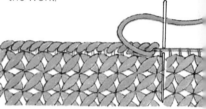

10 Work overcasting stitch in leaf green along both short edges of the rug to cover the folded canvas edges.

12 Steam press and pull into shape.

Needlework

Traditional Sampler

This beautiful sampler not only makes an attractive addition to a room but also includes a variety of stitches to test your embroidery skills.

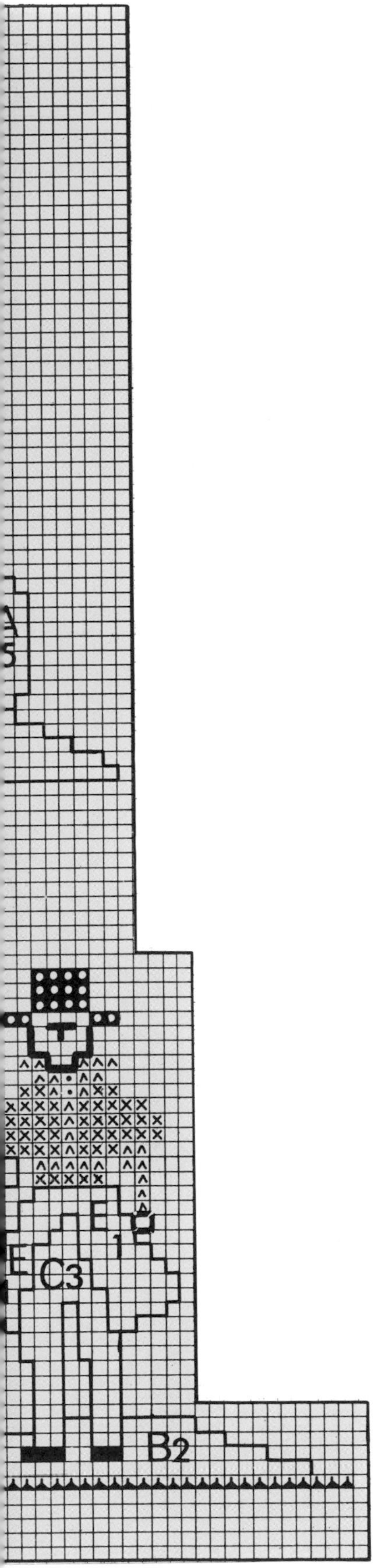
C3
B2

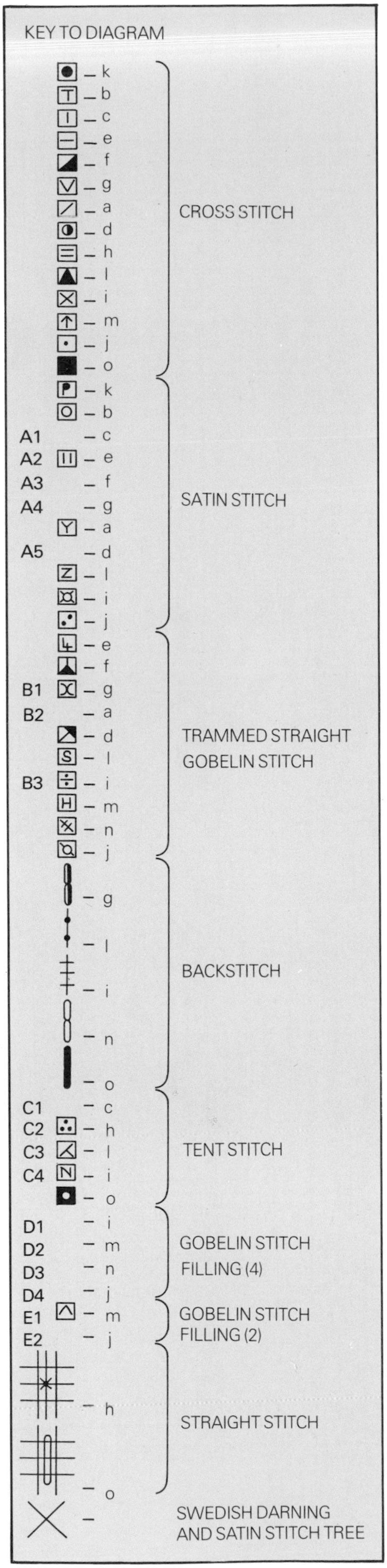
KEY TO DIAGRAM
– k
– b
– c
– e
– f
– g
– a
– d
– h
– l
– i
– m
– j
– o
CROSS STITCH
– k
– b
A1 – c
A2 – e
A3 – f
A4 – g
– a
A5 – d
– l
– i
– j
SATIN STITCH
– e
– f
B1 – g
B2 – a
– d
– l
B3 – i
– m
– n
– j
TRAMMED STRAIGHT GOBELIN STITCH
– g
– l
– i
– n
– o
BACKSTITCH
C1 – c
C2 – h
C3 – l
C4 – i
– o
TENT STITCH
D1 – i
D2 – m
D3 – n
D4 – j
GOBELIN STITCH FILLING (4)
E1 – m
E2 – j
GOBELIN STITCH FILLING (2)
– h
– o
STRAIGHT STITCH
–
SWEDISH DARNING AND SATIN STITCH TREE

Finished size
23 × 15in (58.5 × 38cm).

Materials

¾yd (.6m) of 59in (150cm)-wide evenweave fabric with 21 threads to 1in (2.5cm)
Stranded embroidery floss in the following colors and quantities: 3 skeins light moss green (a); 2 skeins each cerise (b), peacock blue (c), dark moss green (d), light laurel green (e), dark laurel green (f), parrot green (g), orange (h), cinnamon (i), white (j); 1 skein each cardinal red (k), chestnut brown (l), light gray (m), dark gray (n), black (o)
Scroll frame with 27in (68cm) tapes
No. 20 and no. 24 tapestry needles
Piece of stiff cardboard slightly larger than finished embroidery
Strong thread

1 Cut a piece of fabric 27½ × 23½in (70 × 60cm).
2 Mark the center of the fabric, both lengthwise and widthwise, with two lines of basting.
3 Mount the fabric in the frame, with short edges on the tapes.
4 The diagrams on these pages and the next give a little more than half the design. Match the two sections together to obtain the complete diagram. The center lines are indicated by blank arrows. When working, match these marked lines with the lines of basting on the fabric.
5 Each background square on this diagram represents two fabric threads.
6 The numbers in the brackets in the key, represent the number of threads the stitch is worked over.
7 Begin working at the center of the design, 13 threads down from and one thread to the right of the crossed lines of basting, working cross stitch in dark laurel green (f).
8 Work the left side of the sampler given in the two diagrams, omitting the tree and following the diagram and key for the correct colors and stitches. Instructions for working the stitches are given on page 112.
9 Use six strands of embroidery floss when working Swedish darning. Use four strands for trammed straight gobelin stitch, tent stitch, satin stitch and straight stitch. Use three strands for cross stitch and gobelin stitch filling. Use two strands for backstitch.
10 Use the no. 24 tapestry needle when working with two, three and four strands of floss and the no. 20 tapestry needle when working with six strands.
11 When working gobelin stitch filling areas over four fabric threads, work the stitches horizontally. When working over two fabric threads, work the stitches vertically.

John Hutchinson

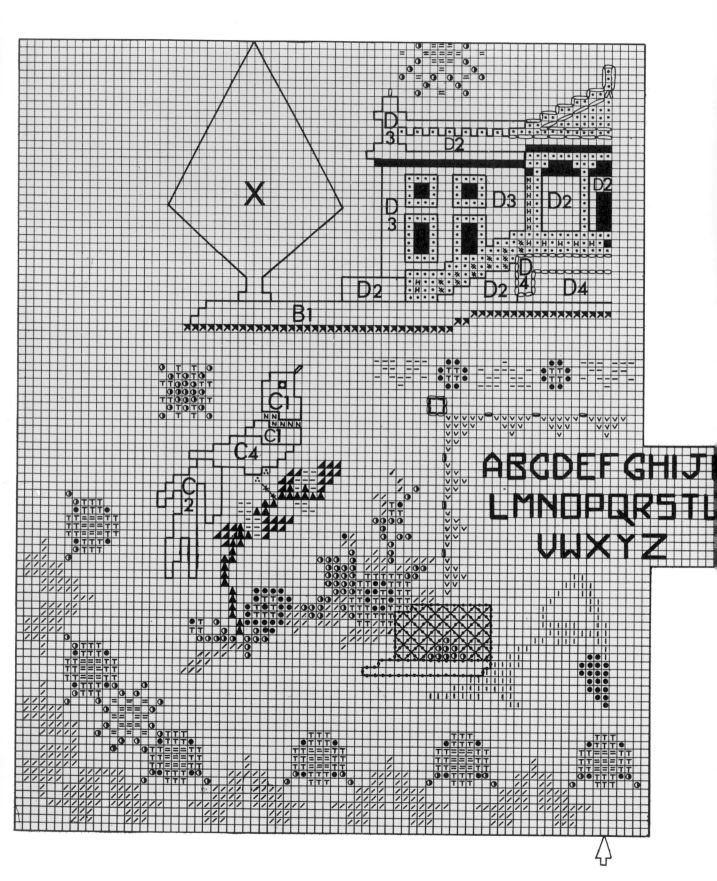

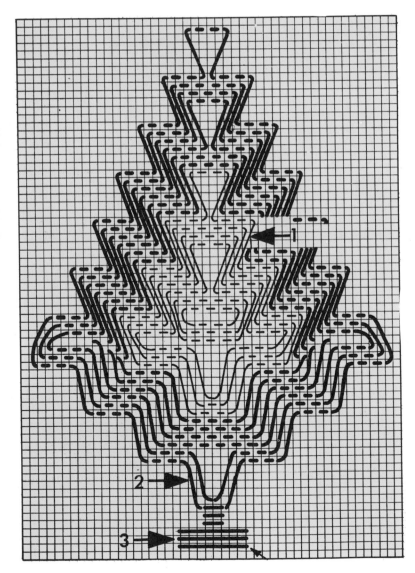

12 On the sides of the basket handle, the front of the main building and the tree trunk the trammed straight gobelin stitches are worked horizontally. All the other trammed straight gobelin stitch is worked vertically.

13 The backstitch on the portico is superimposed on the white cross stitch.

14 Repeat the design in reverse from the blank arrow at the center of the lower edge, omitting the areas already worked.

15 Continue the border around the four sides.

16 To complete the design, work the two trees, following the diagram and key on the left and below. Unlike those in the main diagram, the background lines on this one represent the threads of the fabric.

17 When the embroidery is complete, press it well on the wrong side.

18 Center the embroidery over the board with the right side uppermost and fasten it to the board by sticking pins into the edge of the board. Fold back the surplus fabric and lace it both lengthwise and widthwise with strong thread. Remove the pins.

19 Have the embroidery framed.

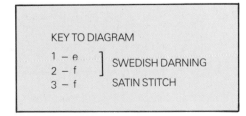

KEY TO DIAGRAM

1 – e ⎤
2 – f ⎦ SWEDISH DARNING
3 – f   SATIN STITCH

Gobelin stitch, filling (4)

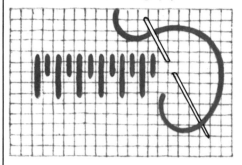

This stitch consists of straight stitches worked in rows alternately from left to right and right to left. Begin the first row by bringing the thread up at the bottom of the line and make a row of stitches alternately over four and two fabric threads. The second row is worked from right to left, with all stitches covering four threads. Continue working each successive row in this way. The spaces left on the last row are filled with stitches worked over two fabric threads, as on the top row.

Gobelin stitch, filling (2)

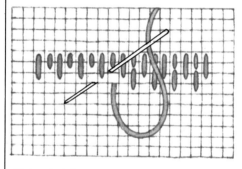

This stitch is worked in the same way as (4), but the stitches are worked over two threads (alternating with stitches over one thread at top and bottom).

Backstitch

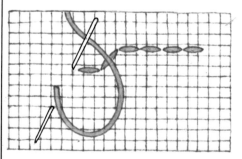

Bring the thread up two fabric threads (or the specific number) in from the starting point. Take it back to the starting point, insert it and bring it out the same distance ahead of the place where the thread first emerged. Continue in this way, working from right to left (or left to right if left-handed).

Straight stitch

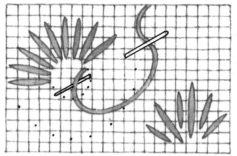

These are single spaced stitches worked either in a regular or irregular manner. Sometimes the stitches are of varying size. The stitches should be neither too long nor too loose.

Tent stitch (continental method)

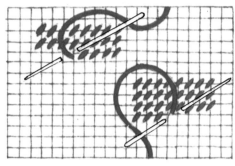

Bring the thread up at the right-hand side; work a stitch diagonally up and to the right over one fabric thread intersection. Pass the needle diagonally downward behind one horizontal and two vertical fabric threads and bring it through ready for the next stitch.
The second row is worked from left to right; the direction of the stitches is the same as the previous row but the needle is passed diagonally upward. The stitches on the reverse side are longer and more sloping than on the right side.

Swedish darning

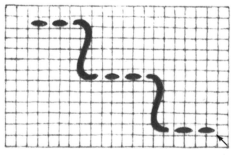

This stitch is worked in rows and can be worked from left to right or from right to left. The order of working the pattern is from the outer rows inward. Begin at the arrow shown in diagram above and weave the thread over and under the desired number of threads.

Cross stitch

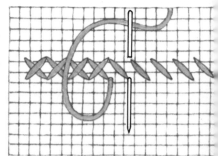

Bring the thread up at the lower right-hand side. Insert the needle two thread[s] up and two threads to the left and bring out again two threads down, forming h[alf] the cross. Continue in this way to the en[d] of the row. Complete the upper half of t[he] cross as shown. This stitch can be work[ed] either from right to left or from left to rig[ht] but it is important that the upper halves [of] all the crosses lie in the same direction t[o] produce a smooth appearance.

Satin stitch

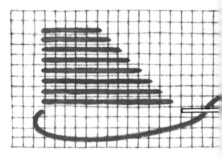

This stitch can be worked either from right to left or from left to right. The number of threads over which this stitch is worked varies considerably, dependin[g] upon the area being worked. When working large areas, use a long thread t[o] avoid having to break it often.

Trammed straight gobelin stitch

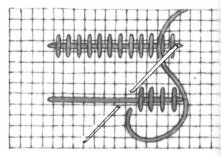

Begin by laying one or more threads be-tween the two horizontal fabric threads to be covered with stitches. These pre-liminary tramming stitches should be no[t] longer than 5in (13cm). Then work straight vertical stitches over the tramming and two fabric threads, from left to right or from right to left.

Homemaker

olstered up

We've made these pillows in all sizes to show the versatility of the bolster. There's a floor cushion, two for the sofa and two to complement a pretty bedroom.

Belinda

Floor cushion

Finished size

About 7½ft (2.3m) long and 16in (40cm) in diameter. A seam allowance of ¾in (2cm) is included.

Materials

3⅛yd (2.8m) of 54in (140cm)-wide firmly-woven fabric
3⅛yd (2.8m) of 54in (140cm)-wide fabric for lining
Paper for pattern; matching thread
Polystyrene beads
Thumbtack; string; pencil

1 Fold a 20in (50cm) square piece of paper evenly into quarters.
2 Tie the string around the pencil; measure and mark 8¼in (21cm) on the string.

3 Tie the free end of the string around the thumbtack, at the mark. Stick the thumbtack into the folded corner of the paper.
4 Keeping the string taut, draw an arc from corner to corner. Keeping the paper folded, cut along the marked line. Unfold the paper pattern.
5 Using the pattern, cut 2 circles from lining fabric. Cut out a piece 94 × 50in (234 × 127cm) for main bolster lining section.

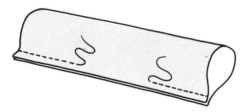

6 Fold main bolster lining section in half lengthwise with right sides together and edges matching. Pin, baste and stitch long edges together, leaving a 30in (75cm) opening in the center of the seam.

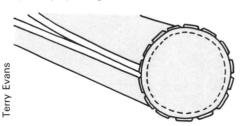

7 Place one lining end circle against one end of main section with right sides

together and edges matching. Pin, baste and stitch in place. Clip the seam allowance.
8 Repeat step 7 at opposite end of main piece. Turn bolster lining right side out.
9 Fill the bolster with polystyrene beads. Do not overfill, so that the bolster will be able to bend into different shapes. Turn in opening edges and slip stitch them firmly together.
10 Repeat steps 5 to 8 to make the bolster cover in the same way.

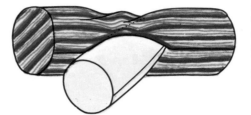

11 Insert the bolster into the bolster cover. Turn in the opening edges and slip stitch them neatly together.

Sofa bolsters

Finished size

About 22in (56cm) long and 8in (20cm) in diameter. A seam allowance of ¾in (2cm) is included.

Materials (for each bolster)

⅝yd (.5m) of 48in (122cm)-wide dark printed fabric
⅝yd (.5m) of 48in (122cm)-wide light printed fabric
⅝yd (.5m) of 36in (90cm)-wide solid-color fabric
3yd (2.7m) of filler cord
1⅛yd (1m) of 36in (90cm)-wide lining fabric
Paper for patterns.
Suitable stuffing; matching thread

1 Make a paper pattern for the end circles as for floor bolster cushion, steps 1 to 4, but with the string only 4¼in (11cm) long.
2 From dark printed fabric cut 2 end circles. Cut one piece 26½ × 7½in (67 × 19cm) for middle section.
3 From light printed fabric cut 2 pieces, each 26½ × 9½ (67 × 24cm), for outer sections.

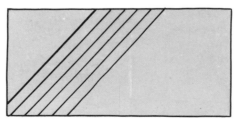

4 From solid-color fabric make a length of cording: cut 2in (5cm)-wide strips on the bias of the fabric. Pin, baste and stitch the

strips together to make a strip 3yd (2.7 long.

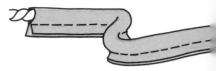

5 Fold the bias strip around the filler co with the wrong side inside. Pin and ba along the complete length, close to the filler cord, to hold it firmly in place.
6 Fold one outer section piece in half widthwise, with right sides together a edges matching. Pin, baste and stitch seam.
7 Repeat step 6 and stitch the other ou section piece into a ring in the same w

8 Fold center section piece in half widthwise, with right sides together a edges matching. Pin, baste and stitch ¾in (2cm) in from each side, leaving center of seam open. Turn right side ou

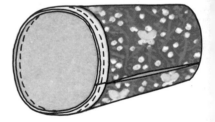

9 Pin the cording to both raw edges of center section, starting at the seam and placing the raw edges together. Cut of the excess cording and sew the ends o the fabric strip together to fit. Baste the cording firmly in place.

10 Pin another length of cording arou one end circle with the cord lying inwa clip into the seam allowance to ease it around the circle. Cut off excess cordi and sew the ends of the fabric strip together to fit. Baste the cording firmly in place.

Terry Evans

11 Repeat step 10 with the other end circle.

12 Place one outer bolster section against one corded edge of center section with seams and edges matching and with right sides together. Pin, baste and stitch in place.

13 Repeat step 12 with other outer bolster section.

14 Place one corded end circle against one end of bolster piece, with right sides together and seams and edges matching. Pin, baste and stitch in place.

15 Repeat step 14 with other end circle piece. Trim seams and turn bolster cover right side out.

16 To make the bolster itself, cut 2 end circles and one piece $26\frac{1}{2} \times 23\frac{1}{2}$in (67 × 60cm).

17 Fold lining main piece in half widthwise with right sides together and edges matching. Pin, baste and stitch long edges, leaving an opening in the center of the seam.

18 Stitch end circle to one end of the bolster, as for cover, step 14.

19 Repeat step 18 to stitch the other end circle in place. Trim seams and turn bolster right side out.

20 Insert stuffing into bolster. Turn in opening edges and slip stitch them together firmly.

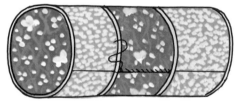

21 Insert bolster into cover. Turn in opening edges and slip stitch together.

Bedroom bolsters

Finished size
About 18in (46cm) long and 7in (18cm) in diameter. A seam allowance of $\frac{3}{4}$in (2cm) is included.

Materials (for each bolster)
1$\frac{3}{8}$yd (1.2m) of 44in (112cm)-wide satin
A bolster of finished size (to make one, see steps 16–20, above)
Two 7in (18cm)-long tassels
Matching thread

1 From satin cut one piece $22\frac{1}{2} \times 27$in (57.5 × 69cm).

2 Fold satin in half lengthwise, with right sides together and edges matching.

Pin, baste and stitch long edges. Turn cover right side out.

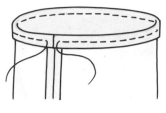

3 Turn in raw edges at each end for $\frac{3}{4}$in (2cm). Pin and baste.

4 Run a line of gathering stitches close to folded edge at one end, leaving the gathering thread hanging free.

5 Repeat step 4 at opposite end of cover.

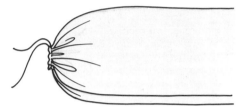

6 Insert bolster into the cover. Pull up gathering thread at each end and fasten off.

7 Place the rosette of one tassel over the gathered end of bolster. Slip stitch in place, covering the gathered end.

8 Repeat step 7 at opposite end of bolster.

9 Repeat steps 1 to 8 to make another bolster in the same way.

Shoestring

Coasters and napkins

Protect your table with these smart coasters with matching napkins

Finished sizes
Each napkin is 8½in (22cm) square.
Each coaster is 4in (10cm) in diameter.

Coaster

Materials
> Two pieces of cotton poplin or glazed cotton fabric, 5in (13cm) square
> Piece of medium-weight interfacing, 5in (13cm) square
> Matching threads
> 14in (35cm) of ½in (1.25cm) bias binding in contrasting color
> Ruler and dressmaker's marking pencil
> Drawing compass or suitable circular object

1 Using a ruler and pencil, divide the right side of both fabric squares into 1in (25cm) squares.
2 Place fabric squares together with wrong sides together and sandwich the interfacing in between.
3 Using a matching thread, topstitch along marked lines through all layers.
4 Cut a 4in (10cm)-diameter circle from the center of each square.
5 Open out the bias binding and press ½in (1.25cm) to wrong side at each end.
6 With right sides together, match the raw edge of the bias binding to the raw edge of the fabric circle.
7 Using thread to match the binding, stitch the binding to the fabric along the binding fold line.
8 Fold the binding over the edge of the circle, slipstitch the ends together and slipstitch the folded edge to the machine stitching on the wrong side of the circle. Press lightly.

Napkin

Materials
> Piece of cotton poplin or glazed cotton fabric, 9in (23cm) square
> Matching and contrasting color sewing threads

1 Using a small, medium-spaced zigzag stitch, sew all around the raw edges of the fabric square.
2 Turn and press a ¼in (5mm) single hem on all edges of the fabric.
3 Using a small, medium-spaced zigzag stitch and contrasting color thread, sew each turning in place. Press well.

Homemaker

et's have a picnic

Give your picnic basket the personal touch—transform a plain hamper into one that's practical as well as pretty, with a place for everything.

Kim Sayer

ned size
rding to size of purchased hamper.

rials
e large hamper-style wicker basket
yd (1.7m) of 36in (90cm)-wide
light printed fabric

3⅜yd (3m) of 36in (90cm)-wide
   dark printed fabric
½yd (.4m) of 36in (90cm)-wide
   polyester batting
6½yd (6m) of ¾in (2cm)-wide white
   eyelet lace edging
11yd (10m) of ¼in (5mm) ribbon

16¼yd (15m) of 1in (2.5cm)-wide
   bias binding
5½yd (5m) of ⅜in (1cm)-wide elastic
1yd (1.1m) of 1in (2.5cm)-wide seam
   binding
10 snaps; matching thread
Tapestry needle

To line the basket lid

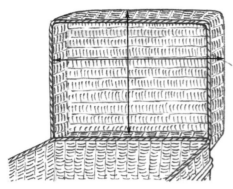

1 Measure the length and width of the basket lid generously. Cut out two pieces of light printed fabric to this size. Cut out one piece of polyester batting to the same size.

2 Place the batting between the two fabric pieces with wrong sides of the fabric inside and edges matching. Pin and baste through all three layers.

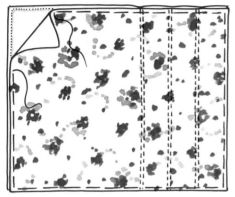

3 Quilt the fabric by stitching parallel double lines, 1½in (4cm) apart, perpendicular to the long sides.

4 Place the quilted fabric inside the lid. Trim it to fit the inside of the lid, allowing ¾in (2cm) of the basket to show on all sides.

5 Finish the raw edges of the quilted fabric with zig-zag stitch.

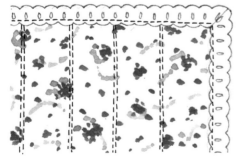

6 Pin and baste the lace edging to the edge of the quilted fabric, placing it right side up, just over the edge, as shown and mitering the corners. Stitch the short edges of the edging together neatly. Stitch the edging in place. Put lid lining to one side.

To line the basket

1 Measure the length and width of the inside base of the basket. Cut out one piece of light printed fabric to this size.

2 Finish the raw edge of the base piece with zig-zag stitch.

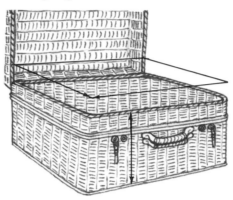

3 Measure the circumference of the basket and the depth of the sides. Add ¾in (2cm) to circumference measurement for side seam. Cut out one side piece this size in light printed fabric.

4 Finish one long edge of side piece with zig-zag stitch.

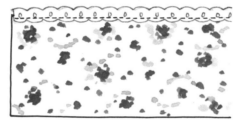

5 Place a length of lace edging on the finished edge of the side piece, placing it on the right side of the fabric, just over the edge. Pin, baste and stitch edging place.

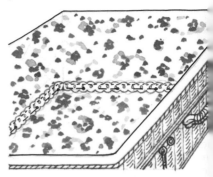

6 Put the base and side pieces in the basket, with the lace edging at the bottom. Fit and pin the two pieces together along the free edge of lace edging.

7 After fitting, pin, baste and stitch the side seam of side piece to fit.

8 Baste and stitch the free long edge o lace edging to base.

9 To mark the top edge of the basket lining, measure from the lower edge a mark off the actual depth less ¾in (2cr to allow for the top lace edging.

10 Trim off excess fabric. Finish the top raw edge with zig-zag stitch.

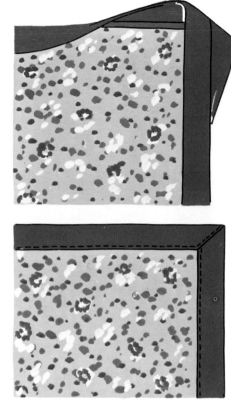

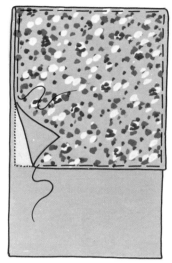

Quilted cutlery bag

1 Cut one piece of dark printed fabric 40 × 14in (100 × 35cm). Cut one piece of batting 16 × 14in (40 × 35cm).

...in and baste a length of lace edging ...e finished long edge of side piece, ...ing edging on the right side of the ...c, just over the edge. Stitch the ...t edges of the edging together to fit. ...ch edging in place. Put basket lining ...ne side.

...lecloth and napkins

...t out one piece of dark printed ...c 36in (90cm) square for tablecloth. ...out four pieces of dark printed fabric, ...n 18in (45cm) square, for napkins. ...nish the edges of the tablecloth and ...n napkin with bias binding. First fold ...ias binding in half lengthwise and ...s.

...arting at one corner of the tablecloth, ...e the wrong side of the binding under ...abric edge, with the tablecloth edge ...ting the center fold of the binding ...own above right.

4 Fold the binding over the raw edge of the tablecloth. Carefully miter the corners: fold the binding at right angles at each corner, then fold the piece to the left of the corner down over the other edge as shown. Pin binding in place.
5 Finish edges at the fourth corner on a diagonal to match the others.
6 Baste and stitch the binding in place, close to the edge of the binding.
7 Repeat steps 2 to 6 to bind each edge of each napkin in the same way.

2 Place the batting on the wrong side of the fabric piece, 8in (20cm) from one short edge. Fold the rest of the fabric down over the batting to cover it, as shown. Pin and baste the three layers together.
3 Quilt the padded section of the fabric with parallel lines, as for basket lid lining, step 3.
4 Trim the quilted fabric to square the edges.
5 Fold the remaining section of fabric over the quilted fabric with wrong side inside, forming a pocket for the cutlery. Pin the edges in place along the two sides through all layers.

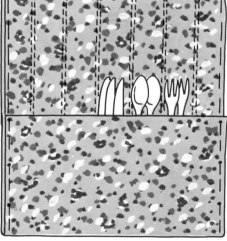

6 Place the cutlery inside the pocket to check the depth. Trim the edge of the pocket so that the tops of the cutlery are visible.
7 Unpin the pocket. Finish the top edge of the pocket with bias binding. First fold the binding in half lengthwise and press.

Terry Evans

121

8 Place the wrong side of the binding under the top pocket edge with the edge at the crease of the binding. Fold the binding over the edge; pin, baste and stitch it in place, close to the edge of the binding.

9 Pin and baste the pocket back in place.

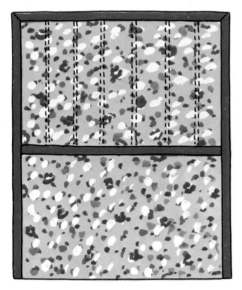

10 To finish the raw edges and to hold the pocket in place, pin, baste and stitch the bias binding around the sides and top of the bag as for the tablecloth, steps 2 to 6. Turn under binding at each side of pocket base to finish the ends.

11 To make the separate compartments for the cutlery: pin, baste and stitch lines through both pocket and quilting. Vary the width of the compartments to accommodate the different sizes of cutlery, can opener, bottle opener and anything else you plan to include.

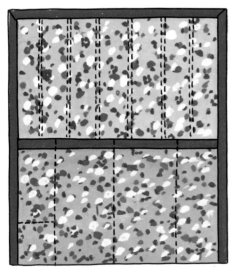

12 For the teaspoons and other short implements, mark and stitch a horizontal line across the pocket to shorten the pocket and prevent the teaspoons from slipping out of sight.

13 To close the bag, fold the quilted top over the cutlery pocket and roll up the bag.

14 To secure the roll, make a tie. Cut a 20in (50cm) length of bias binding. Fold binding in half lengthwise, turning in short edges to finish them. Baste and stitch all along the tie close to the edge.

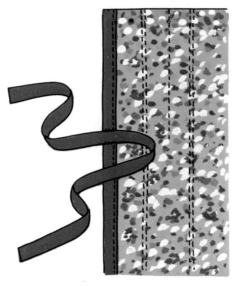

15 Pin and baste the tie to the center of the quilted side of the bag, when the top has been folded down. Sew the tie in place through the bound edge.

Fitting out the basket

1 Mark exactly where the contents will fit in the basket. All the items except the tablecloth and glasses are held in place with strips of fabric-covered elastic.

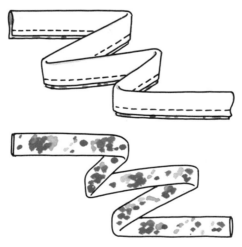

2 Cut out several 2in (5cm)-wide strips of the light printed fabric, long enough to go around picnic items. Fold one strip in half lengthwise with right sides together and edges matching. Pin, baste and stitch down the length, taking $\frac{3}{8}$in (1cm) seam allowance. Turn strip right side out.

3 Repeat step 2 to make the remaining strips in the same way.

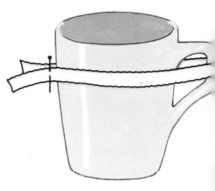

4 For the mugs: measure around one mug, including the handle, with unstretched elastic. Cut off the length.

5 Thread this piece of elastic through [the] fabric strip, securing the elastic at one end with a pin. Stretch the elastic slight[ly] as you work, so that when unstretched it draws the fabric into folds. Secure th[e] elastic at opposite end with a pin. Cut [off] any excess fabric.

6 Join the two ends of the elastic secu[rely.]

7 Turn in the raw ends of the fabric stri[p.] Hand-sew the folded edges together, enclosing the elastic, to form a neat ba[nd] as shown.

8 Repeat steps 4 to 7 to make three mo[re] elasticized strips in the same way for th[e] remaining mugs.

9 Place each elasticized mug band on [the] lining at the right-hand side of the bas[ket.] Determine the correct position by setti[ng a] mug on the base of the basket and wrapping the band around the center of the mug.

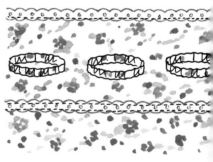

10 Pin, baste and stitch the bands to th[e] lining over their seams forming a $\frac{3}{8}$in (1cm) square of stitching.

and 1½in (4cm) to each side of the center. When in place, the thermos will overlap the cutlery bag.

23 The glasses are held in place on the lid lining with individual strips of seam binding. First measure the circumference of one glass.

Hold the plates in a stack against the [t] of the basket. For the horizontal [d], measure across plates with [st]retched elastic, starting from the [bott]om on one side and ending at the [corr]esponding place under the edges on [o]pposite side.

[D]ivide this measurement in half and [⅜]in (1cm) to each half; this is for [t]wo vertical bands.

[R]epeat steps 5 to 7 to make three [elast]icized straps for the plates, but finish [each] end separately, leaving them as [is].

[P]in and baste the horizontal plate [strap] to the lining, positioning the strap [so th]at it lies across the center of the [plat]es. Stitch each end in place.

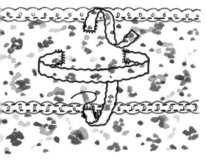

[S]titch the lower vertical strap to the [linin]g at the base of the plate. Hand-sew [at] the center of the horizontal strap. [S]titch the top strap at the top. Sew one [half] of a snap to the point where the [upper] and horizontal straps meet. Sew [the o]ther half to the end of the top strap. [R]epeat steps 11 to 16 to attach the [plates] together in pairs, side by side, to [the b]ack of the basket in the same way as [for th]e plates.

[F]or holding the cutlery bag, cut two [piece]s of elastic to wrap around the [folde]d-up cutlery bag.

[R]epeat step 13 to make the bag straps [in th]e same way as for the plate straps. [S]ew one half of a snap to end of the [cutle]ry bag straps.

[P]osition the cutlery bag straps on the [lid] lining, 2¼in (6cm) from the left-hand [side a]nd 5in (13cm) in from the back and [front] edges.

[R]epeat steps 18 to 21 to make and [stitch] straps in place for the thermos in the [same] way. Position the straps on the left-[hand] side, 2¼in (6cm) from the side edge

24 Cut a piece of seam binding slightly longer than this measurement. Pin, baste and stitch the binding together with a flat seam to form a band.

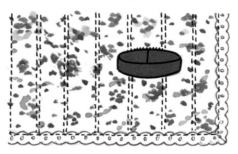

25 Position the band on the lid lining, about 4¼in (11cm) up from lower edge and 2in (5cm) in from right-hand side. Pin, baste and stitch the band in place for ¾in (2cm) to each side of the seam.
26 Repeat steps 23 to 25 to make and stitch three more bands in place, in pairs, one pair on top of the other, spacing them as appropriate for glasses.
27 To hold the tablecloth and napkins make straps from matching fabric. Cut two strips, each 27 × 2in (69 × 5cm).
28 Fold one fabric strip in half lengthwise with right sides together and edges matching. Pin, baste and stitch down the length, taking ⅜in (1cm) seam allowance. Turn strap right side out. Turn in short edges and hand-sew them together.
29 Repeat step 28 to make the other strap.
30 Position one strap vertically on the lid lining, 4in (10cm) from the left-hand side and equidistant from top and bottom. Pin, baste and stitch strap in place for 3½in (9cm) to each side of center point.
31 Position the other strap horizontally across the first strap with centers matching. Pin, baste and stitch in place for 2in (5cm) to each side of the center. Adjust the length as required.
32 Sew one half of a snap to each end of the vertical strap (see drawing). Sew one half of a second snap to the lower end of the vertical strap and the opposite half to the left-hand end of the horizontal

strap.

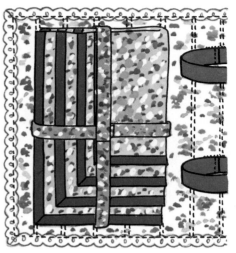

33 Sew one half of the third snap to the underside of the left-hand horizontal strap and half to the right-hand end of the horizontal strap.

To fit the linings into the basket

1 Place the lid lining in the lid. Thread ribbon through the lace edging and through the basket weave using a tapestry needle. Tie off the ends of the ribbon neatly at one corner.
2 Repeat step 1 to fix the base lining in place, inserting ribbon through both lengths of edging.
3 Fit the picnic items in the basket.

Bagged for the beach

Choose cotton canvas in bright colors for this tough and practical beach bag.

Finished size
19in (48cm) deep × 26½in (68cm) all round.

Materials
- One 10¼in (26cm) × 27½in (70cm) piece of canvas fabric in each of bright blue and sea blue
- Two 5¼in (13.5cm) × 5½in (14cm) pieces of canvas in each of red, yellow and orange, all with a selvage along one 5¼in edge
- One 9in (23cm)-diameter circle in each of brown canvas and thick cardboard
- Matching and contrasting threads
- 12 large metal eyelets and a punch
- 1yd (1m) of bright blue thick cord

1 With right sides together and taking an ½in (1cm) seam, stitch the two blue rectangles together along one long edge. Press the seam open and using contrasting color threads, topstitch close to the seam on either side.

2 With right sides facing and using colors alternately, stitch the red, yellow and orange pieces together to make one long strip so that the selvages all lie on one long edge. Press seam open and using contrasting colored thread, topstitch as before.

3 With both right sides facing you and with lower raw edges matching, baste the pocket strip on top of the bright blue canvas.

4 Fold the bag inside out and stitch the side seam through all layers. Press seam open and topstitch as before.

5 Turn ½in (1cm) to the wrong side

around the top edge of the bag. Topstitch in place using contrasting color thread.

6 With right sides together, baste the brown circle to the lower edge of the bag. Stitch in place through all layers. Clip the seam and press towards the base. Turn the bag to the right side.

7 Place the cardboard circle inside the base to stiffen it (but remember to remove it before washing the bag).

8 Position one large eyelet ½in (1cm) from either side of the bag's side seam and 3in (8cm) below the top edge. Position other eyelets at approximately 2in (5cm) intervals around the circumference of the bag.

9 Thread the cord through the eyelets and tie across the side seam. Knot each end of the cord and fray slightly to form tassels.

homemaker

This comfortable quilted seat cleverly converts into a twin bed, perfect for an overnight guest.

hair-bed

Finished size 35 × 30in (90 × 75cm).
14in (35cm) deep.
A seam allowance of $\frac{3}{4}$in (2cm) is included.

Materials
  6yd (5.5m) of 50in (128cm)-wide upholstery fabric
  6yd (5.5m) of 45in (115cm)-wide fabric for backing
  1yd (1.3m) of 36in (90cm)-wide lightweight batting
  Two foam cushions 36 × 30in (90 × 66cm) and 7in (18cm) thick
  Foam chips for headrest
  Matching and contrasting thread
  Paper for pattern; tailor's chalk

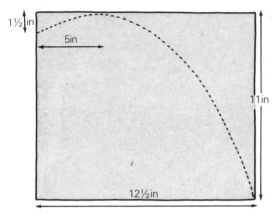

1 Make a paper pattern for the side of the headrest: on a sheet of paper draw a rectangle 12½ × 11in (32 × 28cm). Measuring from one corner, mark a point 5in (13cm) along the longer side and another point 1½in (4cm) along the shorter side. Join these points together with a curved line as shown, continuing the line smoothly to the corner diagonally opposite the first. Cut out the resulting pattern.
2 Cut out all the pieces from the main fabric, following the appropriate cutting layout on page 128 for measurements.
3 Cut out all the pieces from backing fabric following the appropriate cutting layout on page 128 for measurements.
4 Using backing fabric pieces as patterns, cut out pieces A, C, D and E from double batting; cut B and F (gussets and headrest sides) from a single thickness.

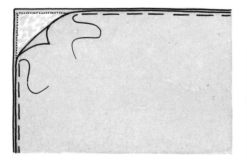

5 Place all three "A" pieces together, with the batting sandwiched between

the main fabric and the backing fabric. Pin and baste around all four edges.
6 Repeat step 5 to baste all the pieces together in threes.

7 Mark quilting lines on the main piece, using tailor's chalk. On the right side, mark the lines 6in (15cm) apart across the width and down the length of the fabric. Mark the first line 6¾in (17cm) from the raw edges.

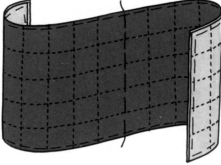

8 Baste along each quilting line. Using a larger-than-average stitch, machine stitch along each basted line using contrasting thread, omitting the line that runs across the width of the fabric at the center.
9 Repeat steps 7 and 8 with cushion base, this time stitching all the quilting lines.
10 Repeat steps 7 and 8 on seat top, but begin the widthwise lines 2¾in (7cm) from one short edge. Mark, but do not stitch the next widthwise line.
11 Place the main piece and seat top together, with wrong sides facing and with their respective unstitched quilting lines matching, as shown below. When stitched, these lines will form the "hinge" of the chair-bed.

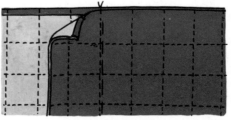

12 Turn under ¾in (2cm) at the side edges of both pieces; press. Pin, baste and stitch

together through all thicknesses on th[e] marked quilting line, using contrastin[g] sewing thread.
13 Mark and stitch quilting lines as before, on headrest; begin the quiltin[g] lines 6¾in (17cm) from one long edge [and] end 3¼in (8cm) from opposite long e[dge.]

14 Place one headrest side piece agai[nst] headrest top, with right sides and sho[rt] edges together and with the edge wit[h] complete squares to the front, along t[he] slope. Pin, baste and stitch together.
15 Repeat step 14 to attach the other headrest side piece.

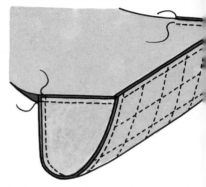

16 Place complete headrest at the lon[g] free edge of seat top, with right sides [together] together and edges matching, as sho[wn.] Pin, baste and stitch side edges and o[ne] long edge. Turn headrest right side ou[t.] Leave remaining seam open for stuffi[ng.]
17 Place one short edge of cushion b[ase] opposite end of seat top. Pin, baste a[nd] stitch together.
18 Clip the seam allowance on each s[ide] of the center quilted line on the main section, ⅜in (1cm) from stitching line[.]

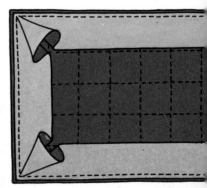

19 Place one long edge of one gusse[t to] one half of main piece. Pin one shor[t]

of gusset to center of main piece. Continue pinning down the side, along the end and up to opposite side of center. Baste and stitch in place, starting and ending at clip in seam allowance.

20 Repeat step 19 to join the other gusset piece to the opposite half of the main piece.

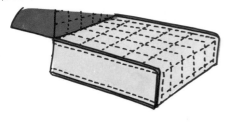

21 On one side, pin, baste and stitch end of gusset to seat top.

Continue stitching the remaining long edge of gusset to the seat top, leaving the back seam open.

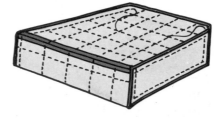

22 Pin, baste and stitch remaining long edge of other gusset to lower front of cushion base, leaving back seam open for stuffing.
23 Trim seam; turn cover right side out.
24 Insert a piece of foam into each

cushion section. Turn in the opening edges ¾in (2cm) on cushion base. Slip stitch edges firmly together.

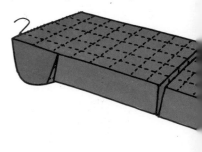

25 Fill headrest with foam chips. Turn ¾in (2cm) on free edge of seat top; lap this edge over free edge of headrest. P baste and slip stitch folded edge in pla

Key to layout for 50in and 45in-wide fabric

A Main piece
B Gusset
C Seat top
D Cushion base
E Headrest
F Headrest side

Cutting layout for 50in-wide fabric.

Cutting layout for 45in-wide fabric.

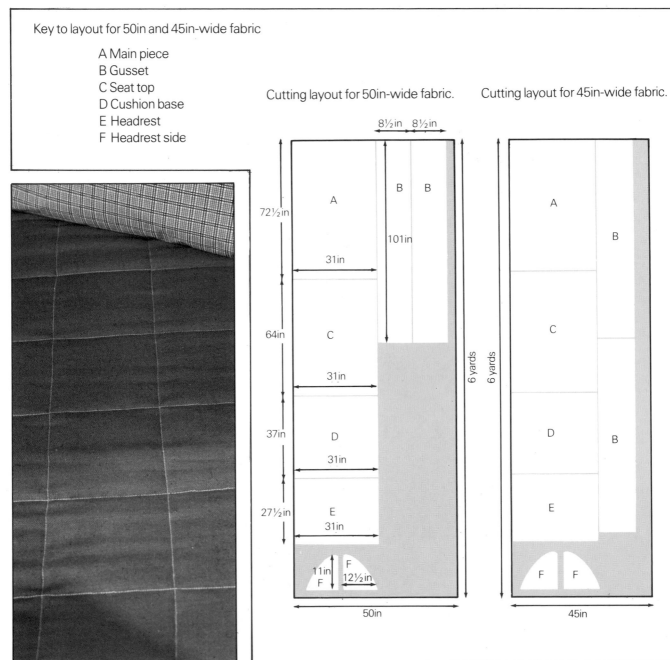